# Rudiments of Anglo-Saxon

## Answer Key

Published by Canon Press
P.O. Box 8729, Moscow, ID 83843
800-488-2034 | www.canonpress.com

Douglas Wilson, *Rudiments of Anglo Saxon:* Answer Key


Layout design by Lucy Zoe Jones
Printed in the United States of America.



Library of Congress Cataloging-in-Publication Data

Wilson, Douglas, 1953-
Anglo-Saxon rudiments : answer key / Douglas Wilson.
p. cm.
ISBN 978-1-59128-085-9
1. English language--Old English, ca. 450-1100. 2. English language--Old English, ca. 450-1100--Grammar. I. Title.

PE135.W556 2012
429'.82076--dc23

2011036520

12 13 14 15 16 17 18 19 20 10 9 8 7 6 5 4 3 2 1

# Rudiments of Anglo-Saxon

An Introductory Guide to Old English
for Christian and Home Schools
Answer Key

**Douglas Wilson**

canonpress
Moscow, Idaho

# Table of Contents

UNIT ONE

# GRAMMAR RUDIMENTS

[This page intentionally left blank]

# Chapter 1

# Alphabet & Pronunciation

## 1.2 Vocabulary Exercises

Translate the following phrases into Anglo-Saxon. But as you do, remember that you don't actually know that much yet. If you haven't learned how to translate paltry words like *the* and *in*, just use Modern English; we'll get to the rest in good time. And some of you grammar junkies may be wondering about how to match the nouns and adjectives in gender, case and number, but again, don't worry about it for now.

1. dark daughter — blæc/mirce/deorc/dimm dohtor
2. verbose historian — wordig wyrdwritere
3. fair maiden — fæger mæden
4. world made of glass — glæsen eorðe/middangeard
5. weak game — unmihtig gamen
6. unloved arithmetic — freondleas rimcræft
7. impure odor — unclænlic stenc
8. just as a large peg — swa swa a great pinn
9. hard nail — heard nægl
10. ice pail — is pægel
11. fatherly earl — fæderlic ealdorman
12. dim abode of the dead — dimm deaðwic
13. a kernel in the earth — a cyrnel in the earðe/grund/middangeard
14. the large hammer in the raid — the great homer in the rad
15. a saddle on the sand — sadol in the sond
16. ghost's bane — gæst's bana
17. a beacon in the camp protected by water — a beacen in the wæterfæsten
18. an acre of corn — an æcer of corn
19. baby of the family — bearn/cradolcild of the cynn
20. a demonic foe in the hall of ancient duty — a scyn-scaþa in the heall of ealdriht

## Exercise B

Take the following Modern English words and write them using Anglo-Saxon phonetics. In other words, write them the way Beowulf would if he heard the word *thicket* and was taking a stab at the spelling. If you happen to know the Anglo-Saxon word for one of these, don't write *that* down. The exercise is simply to duplicate the sound.

1. thicket — Þiket
2. same — sēm
3. burden — burdin
4. thin — Þin
5. castle — cæssul
6. bucket — buket
7. edge — ecg
8. torrent — tōrint
9. harden — hardin
10. book — buk
11. can — can
12. music — mūsic
13. with — wiþ
14. sword — sōrd
15. God — God
16. master — mæsstur
17. tree — trī
18. computer — compūtur
19. cabin — cæbin
20. whale — wēl
21. gold — gōld
22. silver — silfur
23. shelf — scelf
24. the — ðe
25. standard — standurd
26. stone — stōn
27. brick — bric
28. wood — wud
29. spear — spyr
30. mark — mark
31. car — car
32. boat — bōt
33. bird — burd
34. frog — frog
35. distance — disstans
36. weird — wyrd
37. fan — fan
38. nut — nut
39. pin — pin
40. sledge — slecg
41. baby — bēbig
42. fish — fisc
43. ship — scip
44. paint — pēnt
45. gum — gum
46. string — strīng
47. children — cildrin
48. lovely — luflig
49. hate — hēt
50. pig — pig

## 1.5 Quiz

### Alphabet (10 points)

1. What does the letter *thorn* look like? Þ
2. What sound does it make? th in thigh
3. What does the letter *eth* look like? ð
4. What sound does it make? th in thy
5. How should you pronounce the two d's in *biddan*? pronounce them both
6. What sound does an *f* make in the middle of a word? v
7. What sound does an *s* make in the middle of a word? z
8. What does the letter *ash* look like? æ
9. What sound does it make? a in sat
10. What sound does an *sc* make? sh

### Translate from Anglo-Saxon to English (2 points each)

11. stormsæ — tempest
12. dead — dead
13. wyrdwritere — historian
14. glæsen — made of glass
15. nægl — nail
16. sond — sand
17. ealdriht — ancient duty
18. freondleas — unloved
19. bana — bane
20. rad — raid
21. mirce — dark
22. is — ice
23. fyll — fall
24. hlæder — ladder
25. ealdorman — earl
26. middangeard — middle yard, middle earth
27. healf — half
28. fæderlic — fatherly
29. aweccan — to waken
30. rimcræft — arithmetic

### Translate from English to Anglo-Saxon (2 points each)

31. acer — æcer
32. fair — fæger
33. verbose — wordig
34. darling — deorling
35. to bake — bacan
36. hammer — homor
37. fat — fætt
38. queen — cwen
39. bastard — bastard
40. abode of the dead — deaðwic
41. hardness — heardnes
42. beacon — beacen
43. calf — cealf
44. camp protected by water — wæterfæsten

## Translate from English to Anglo-Saxon (continued):

45. salty — sealt
46. earring — earhring
47. to rise — uppian
48. kernel — cyrnel
49. earth — earðe, grund, middangeard
50. baby — bearn, cradolcild

## Fill in the blanks (10 points).

51.

**Fæder** ure þu þe eart on **heofonum** , si þin name gehalgod.
To becume þin **rice** , gewurþe ðin willa on **eorðan** swa on heofonum.
Urne **gedæghwamlican** hlaf syle us todæg,
And **forgyf** us ure gyltas swa swa we forgyfað urum **gyltendum** .
And ne **gelæd** þu us on **costnunge** ac alys us of yfele. **Soþlice** (Luke 11:2-4)

# Chapter 2

# Verb Rudiments

## 2.2 Vocabulary Exercises

Translate the following phrases into Anglo-Saxon. Again, if you don't know how to say a certain word in Anglo-Saxon, just use the Modern English equivalent.

1. candle in the east —tapor in the east
2. the deacon of the people — the diacon of the folc
3. sardine on Saturday — smelt on Sæternesdæg
4. wicked satisfaction — yfel bliss
5. a deep pan — a deop panne
6. glass harp — glæs hearpe
7. beer in bed — beor in bedd/ræst/bedrest
8. the quick hare — the swift hara
9. baptism of the hero on Sunday — fulluht of the brego on Sunnandæg/Haligdæg
10. deed of the god — dæd of the god
11. a glad earwig — a glæd earwicga
12. the least harm — the læst hearm
13. rain on the fen — regn on the fenn
14. the verse on the wall — the fers on the weall
15. to make fast a camp protected by woods — fæsten a wudefæsten
16. to send the wicked man to jail — sendan the yfel mon to carcern
17. a tale of the oak made of gold — a talu of the gylden ac
18. the sailor in the accident last night — the flotman in the belimp toniht
19. the cauldron at the entrance — the citel at the ingang
20. the name of the wary person on the warm sandy beach —
    the nama of the wær mon on the wearm sondlond

## 2.4 Grammar Exercises

### Exercise A

Complete the chart for the followings verbs

| | **standan** |
|---|---|
| Infinitive | standan—to stand |
| First | stande |
| Second | stentst |
| Third | stent |
| Plural | standaþ |

| | **ridan** |
|---|---|
| Infinitive | ridan |
| First | ride |
| Second | ridest |
| Third | rideþ |
| Plural | ridaþ |

| | **feohtan** |
|---|---|
| Infinitive | feohtan—to fight |
| First | feohte |
| Second | fiehtst |
| Third | fieht |
| Plural | feohtaþ |

| | **beran** |
|---|---|
| Infinitive | beran |
| First | bere |
| Second | birst |
| Third | birþ |
| Plural | berað |

| | **folgian** |
|---|---|
| Infinitive | folgian |
| First | folgie |
| Second | folgast |
| Third | folgaþ |
| Plural | folgiaþ |

## Exercise B

Write "strong" or "weak" next to each Modern English verb. The easiest way to do this is to take each verb, move it to the past tense, and see whether you added the ending "*-ed*" (weak) or changed the stem entirely (strong).

1. I like. — weak
2. He strikes. — strong
3. We mind. — weak
4. They arrive. — weak
5. You deride. — weak
6. I argue. — weak
7. I tell. — strong
8. They fake. — weak
9. We cook. — weak
10. I sit. — strong
11. He sings. — strong
12. You drive. —strong
13. We bake. — weak
14. I write. —strong
15. I shoot. — strong
16. You run. — strong
17. We walk. — weak
18. I fight. — strong
19. I swim. — strong
20. It flies. — strong

## Exercise C

Write the Anglo-Saxon for each of these simple sentences. Keep in mind that, in the plural, you won't have the full sense without the pronouns; those will come later. This means that, for now, you will be correct if you write *feohtaþ* to mean *they fight* as well as *we fight.*

1. You come. — cymst
2. They rode. — ridon
3. He carries. — birþ
4. She comes. — cymþ
5. I follow. — folgie
6. You (all) fight. — feohtaþ
7. He stands. — stent
8. I fight. — feohte
9. They carry. — berað
10. I rode. — rad
11. We fight. — feohtaþ
12. You followed. — folgodest
13. You fight. — fiehtst
14. We come. — cumaþ
15. You follow. — folgast
16. You bear. — birst
17. You fight. — fieht
18. They follow. — folgiaþ
19. We carry. — berað
20. I followed. — folgode

### Exercise D

A macaronic exercise is one where two different languages are jumbled together. It can be quite helpful if you don't really know enough words yet to do much in your new language. (Take note, however, that this exercise is not quite macaronic because both languages are English—after a fashion.) With that in mind, complete the sentences by filling in the blanks with the best Anglo-Saxon option.

1. John **fieht** the battle.
2. Henry **birþ** the sack.
3. Paul **stent** firm.
4. They had **folgodon** the footsteps.
5. He **cymþ** when he is called.
6. You all **standaþ** still.
7. We **ridonour** horses yesterday.
8. The boys **folgiaþ or folgodon** their guide.
9. We **feohtaþ** the war.
10. King Charles **birþ** the scepter.

## 2.5 Quiz

### Grammar of Verbs (10 points)

1. How many tenses are there in Anglo-Saxon? — two
2. What are they? — present and past/preterite
3. What is the name for what we call helping verbs? — preterite-present
4. What is the distinguishing feature of weak verbs? — they are predictable in the stem, and move from the present tense to the past tense simply by adding to the end of the word.
5. What is the distinguishing feature of strong verbs? — the move from the present tense to the past tense by altering in the stem, changing the vowel sound.
6. How many principal parts does a weak verb have? — three
7. How many principal parts does a strong verb have? — four
8. Does Anglo-Saxon have a past continuous? — no
9. Counting the infinitive, how many words do you list when you conjugate a verb in one tense? — five: infinitive, first singular, second singular, third singular, plural.
10. In how many columns? — one

## Meaning of Verbs (6 points)

11. What does *ridan* mean? — to ride
12. What does *feohtan* mean? — to fight
13. What does *cuman* mean? — to come
14. What does *folgian* mean? — to follow
15. What does *standan* mean? — to stand
16. What does *beran* mean? — to bear

## Translate (24 points)

Translate the following into Modern English, including the correct pronoun. With the plural, you may pick your pronoun.

17. feohte — I fight
18. folgast — you follow
19. folgode — he/she/it followed
20. rideþ — he/she/it rides
21. rad — I/he/she/it rode
22. ride — I ride/you rode
23. folgodon — we/you all/they followed
24. cumaþ — we/you all/they come
25. ridaþ — we/you all/they ride
26. folgodest — you followed
27. birþ — he/she/it bears
28. birst — you bear
29. folgiaþ — we/you all/they follow
30. feohtaþ — we/you all/they fight
31. fieht — he/she/it fights
32. stande — I stand
33. folgie — I follow
34. stent — he/she/it stands
35. cume — I come
36. folgaþ — he/she/it follows
37. fiehtst — you fight
38. berað — we/you all/they bear
39. stentst — you stand
40. bere — I bear

## Translate (25 points)

Translate from Anglo-Saxon to Modern English

41. east — east
42. earwicga — earwig
43. deop — deep
44. hearm — harm
45. gylden — made of gold
46. ræst — bed
47. finger — finger
48. beforan — before
49. hearpe — harp
50. carcern — jail
51. dæd — deed
52. fers — verse
53. folc — people
54. hearpian — to play the harp

55. nacod — naked
56. tapor — candle
57. swift — quick
58. hand — hand
59. sceab — scab
60. ealdriht — ancient duty
61. wæterfæsten — camp protected by water
62. dohtor — daughter
63. fæderlic — fatherly
64. cwen — queen
65. cradolcild — baby

## Translate (25 points):

Translate from Modern English to Anglo-Saxon (25 points)

66. beer — beor
67. fe — fæge
68. glad — glæd
69. god — god
70. kettle — cytel
71. warm — wearm
72. camp protected by woods — wudefæsten
73. Saturday — Sæternesdæg
74. entrance — ingang
75. name — nama
76. mane — manu
77. least — læst
78. sailor — flotman
79. wicked — yfel
80. to make fast — fæstan
81. cauldron — citel
82. sandy beach — sondlond
83. accident — belimp
84. satisfaction — bliss
85. made of glass — glæsen
86. tempest — stormsæ
87. historian — wyrdwritere
88. unloved — freondleas
89. arithmetic — rimcræft
90. hammer — hamor

## Fill in the blanks (10 points):

91.

**Fæder** ure þu þe eart on heofonum, si þin **name** gehalgod. To **becume** þin rice, **gewurþe** ðin willa on eorðan swa on heofonum. Urne **gedæghwamlican** hlaf syle us todæg, And forgyf us ure **gyltas** swa swa we **forgyfað** urum gyltendum. And ne gelæd þu us on costnunge ac **alys** us of **yfele**. **Soþlice**. (Luke 11:2-4)

# Chapter 3

# Noun Rudiments

## 3.2 Vocabulary Exercises

### Translate the following phrases into Anglo-Saxon.

1. the fin in the water — the finn in the wæter
2. behind the den — behindan the denn
3. to kill fifty gnats — cwellan fiftig gnæts
4. to glide through the deep pool — glidan through the wæl
5. the key in the icy marsh — the cæg in the isig mersc
6. seed of a pear — sæd/corn of a peru
7. shadow in the temple — sceadu in the tempul
8. weapon made of lindenwood — wæpn linden
9. to yell everywhere — giellan æg-hwear
10. the risk of famine on the beach — the pliht of hungor on the strand
11. hart in the harvest — heorot in the harvest
12. wickedness of the harlot — yfelnes of the hore
13. to tell of the bucktoothed but clever acolyte

    — tellan of the twiseltoþ but snotor candelbora
14. to begin another Easter Sunday — beginnan oðer Easterdæg
15. everyone under the plaster — æg-hwa under the plaster
16. fifteen fleas on the cat — fiftiene fleas on the catt
17. to read the Danelaw — rædan the Denelagu
18. pea, leek, and onion — pise, leac and leac
19. the mare on the seawall — the myre on the sæweall
20. the goad of mankind — the gad of moncynn

## 3.4 Grammar Exercises

### Exercise A

Complete the charts for the various nouns.

**scip**

| | Singular | Plural |
|---|---|---|
| **Nominative** | scip | scipu |
| **Genetive** | scipes | scipa |
| **Dative** | scipe | scipum |
| **Accusative** | scip | scipu |

**hand**

| | Singular | Plural |
|---|---|---|
| **Nominative** | hand | handa |
| **Genetive** | handa | handa |
| **Dative** | handa | handum |
| **Accusative** | hand | handa |

**nama**

| | Singular | Plural |
|---|---|---|
| **Nominative** | nama | naman |
| **Genetive** | naman | namena |
| **Dative** | naman | namum |
| **Accusative** | naman | naman |

Complete the charts for the various nouns.

**wela**

| | Singular | Plural |
|---|---|---|
| Nominative | wela | welan |
| Genetive | welan | walena |
| Dative | welan | welum |
| Accusative | welan | welan |

**guma**

| | Singular | Plural |
|---|---|---|
| Nominative | guma | guman |
| Genetive | guman | gumena |
| Dative | guman | gumum |
| Accusative | guman | guman |

**wer**

| | Singular | Plural |
|---|---|---|
| Nominative | wer | weras |
| Genetive | weres | wera |
| Dative | were | werum |
| Accusative | wer | weras |

## Exercise B

Complete the sentences by filling in the blanks with the best Anglo-Saxon option. That means paying attention to your case endings.

1. The **wer/guma** married the woman. (nominative singular)
2. The dragon lay curled on top of its great pile of **welan**. (dative singular)
3. The **naman** of the warriors were Beowulf and Wiglaf. (nominative plural)
4. The cargo was carried aboard the only **scipe** in the harbor. (dative singular)
5. Many **handa** make light work. (nominative plural)
6. The **weras/guman** were armed with swords and ready to fight. (nominative plural)
7. Her **nama** was Ellen. (nominative singular)
8. Helen of Troy launched a thousand **scipu**. (accusative plural)
9. On one **handa** he wore a gold ring. (dative singular)
10. They robbed the **wer/guman** of his money. (accusative singular)

## 3.5 Quiz

### Fill out the appropriate endings. (15 points).

1.

| | Singular | Plural |
|---|---|---|
| **Nominative** | *nama* | naman |
| **Genetive** | naman | namena |
| **Dative** | naman | namum |
| **Accusative** | naman | naman |

2.

| | Singular | Plural |
|---|---|---|
| **Nominative** | *scip* | scipu |
| **Genetive** | scipes | scipa |
| **Dative** | scipe | scipum |
| **Accusative** | scip | scipu |

### Give an appropriate Anglo-Saxon rendering for each of these sentences. Don't worry about articles (20 points).

3. The names stand. – The naman standaþ.

4. The ships come. – The scipu cumaþ.

5. The hand fights the hands. – The hand fieht the handa.

6. He follows the ship. – He folgaþ the scip.

7. The men carry the wealth. The weras/guman berað the welan.

## Translate from Anglo-Saxon to Modern English (25 points).

8. lust — lust
9. wæl — deep pool
10. gad — goad
11. leac — leak/onion
12. seofon — seven
13. myre — mare
14. oðer — another
15. corn — corn
16. temprian — temper
17. isig — icy
18. strand — beach
19. horsc — harsh
20. sceadu — shadow
21. linden — made of lindenwood
22. giellan — to yell
23. mersc — marsh
24. cræft — craft
25. yfelnes — wickedness
26. finn — fin
27. tellan — to tell
28. Haligdæg — Sunday
29. bliss — satisfaction
30. belimp — accident
31. unclænlic — impure
32. deaðwic — abode of the death

## Translate from Modern English to Anglo-Saxon (25 points).

33. Easter Sunday — Easterdæg
34. to begin — beginnan
35. to read — rædan
36. seawall — sæweall
37. harpstring — hearpestreng
38. mankind — moncynn
39. to glide — glidan
40. glove — glofu
41. seventeen — seofontiene
42. waste — weste
43. weapon — wæpn
44. harvest — hærfest
45. Danelaw — Denelagu
46. risk — pliht
47. beach — strand
48. wax — weax
49. famine — hungor
50. very — ful
51. acolyte — candelbora
52. to yell — giellan
53. wary — wær
54. to get drunk — druncnian
55. people — folc
56. to understand —understandan
57. salty — sealt

## Fill in the blanks (15 points):

58.

Fæder **ure** þu þe **eart** on heofonum, si þin name **gehalgod**.

To becume þin **rice**, gewurþe ðin **willa** , on eorðan swa on **heofonum**.

Urne **gedæghwamlican** hlaf syle us todæg,

And **forgyf** us ure gyltas **swa swa** we forgyfað urum gyltendum.

And ne **gelæd** þu us **on** costnunge **ac** alys us **of** yfele.

**Soþlice**. (Luke 11:2-4)

# Chapter 4

# Pronoun Rudiments

## 4.2 Vocabulary Exercises

### Translate the following phrases into Anglo-Saxon.

1. the better answer — the betera andswaru
2. to bite the bishop — to bitan the biscop
3. the devil's fist — the deofol's fyst
4. the port of Christendom — the port of Cristendom
5. to eat the cheese — etan the ciese
6. bitter blood — biter blod
7. the devilish goat under the fir-tree — the deoflic gat under the furhwudu
8. fish in a flask — fisc in a flaxe
9. anyone in the haven — hywlc in the hæfen
10. to lick each marshmallow — liccian ge-hwylc merscmealuwe
11. old sheep — eald sceap
12. girl of small beauty — mæden of lytel glæm
13. flood on the riverbank — flod on the strand
14. the monk's treasure below the mast — the mynstermonn's hord below the mæst
15. the sky over the peony — the heofan over the peonie
16. to sharpen the flint — scyrpan the flint
17. to reap the agriculture — ripan the eorðtilð
18. five hearts — fif heortes
19. deadly hatred of eels — bealoful hete of æls
20. to pierce the table with an arrow made of stone — stingan the bord with a flan stænen

## 4.4 Grammar Exercises

### Complete the charts for the various pronouns.

1. First Person

| | Singular | Plural |
|---|---|---|
| **Nominative** | ic | we |
| **Genetive** | min | user/ure |
| **Dative** | me | us |
| **Accusative** | me/mec | us/usic |

2. Second Person

| | Singular | Plural |
|---|---|---|
| **Nominative** | þu | ye |
| **Genetive** | þin | eower |
| **Dative** | þe | eow |
| **Accusative** | þe/þec | eow/eowic |

3. Third Person Singular

| | Masculine | Feminine | Neuter |
|---|---|---|---|
| **Nominative** | he | heo | hit |
| **Genetive** | his | hire | his |
| **Dative** | him | hire | him |
| **Accusative** | hine | hie | hit |

4. Third Person Plural

| | Masculine | Feminine | Neuter |
|---|---|---|---|
| **Nominative** | | hie | |
| **Genetive** | | hira | |
| **Dative** | | him | |
| **Accusative** | | hie | |

## 4.5 Quiz

### Translate the following (10 points)

1. ge — you all
2. hie — they
3. ic — I
4. hit — it
5. þu — you
6. he — he
7. heo — she
8. we — we
9. hira —theirs
10. eowic — you (all)

### Using pronouns (even when unnecessary), write the equivalent of these sentences (10 points)

11. They bear. — Hie berað.
12. She follows. — Heo folgaþ.
13. We stand. — We standaþ.
14. They stand. — Hie standaþ.
15. She rides. — Heo rideþ.
16. You rode. — Þu ride.
17. He follows. — He folgaþ.
18. It fights. — Hit fieht.
19. You all come. — Ge cumaþ.
20. We ride. — We ridaþ.

### Translate the following Anglo-Saxon to English (5 points)

21. folgie. — I follow.
22. Þu folgast. — You follow.
23. Ic folgie. — I follow.
24. folgaÞ. — He/She/It follows.
25. Heo folgaÞ. — She follows.

## 26. Fill in the following paradigm (7 points)

| | Singular | Plural |
|---|---|---|
| **Nominative** | ic | we |
| **Genetive** | min | user/ure |
| **Dative** | me | us |
| **Accusative** | me/mec | us/usic |

## 27. And again (7 points)

| | Singular | Plural |
|---|---|---|
| **Nominative** | þu | ge |
| **Genetive** | þin | eower |
| **Dative** | þe | eow |
| **Accusative** | þe/þec | eow/eowic |

## 28. And again (9 points)

| | Masculine | Feminine | Neuter |
|---|---|---|---|
| **Nominative** | he | heo | hit |
| **Genetive** | his | hire | his |
| **Dative** | him | hire | him |
| **Accusative** | hine | hie | hit |

## Translate from Anglo-Saxon to Modern English (1 point each)

29. furhwudu — fir-tree
30. scyrpan — sharpen
31. bealoful — deadly
31. blod — blood
33. þanan — thence
34. hæfen — haven
35. stænen — made of stone
36. fyst — fist
37. dwinan — to become small
38. seofontiene — seventeen
39. peru — pear
40. flotman — sailor
41. ingang — entrance
42. leðer — leather
43. earwicga — earwig

## Translate from Modern English to Anglo-Saxon (1 point each)

44. Christendom — Cristendom
45. answer — andswaru
46. marshmallow — merscmealuwe
47. navel — nafela
48. reader — rædere
49. agriculture — eorðtilð
50. devil — deofol
51. monk — mynstermonn
52. arrow — flan
53. treasure — hord
54. seven — seofon
55. marsh — mersc
56. to begin — beginnan
57. wary — wær
58. paradise — paradis

## Fill in the blanks (22 points)

59.

**Fæder ure** þu þe **eart** on heofonum, si **þin** name **gehalgod**.

To **becume** þin **rice**, gewurþe ðin **willa**, on **eorðan** swa on **heofonum**.

Urne **gedæghwamlican** hlaf syle us **todæg**,

And **forgyf** us ure gyltas **swa swa** we forgyfað **urum gyltendum**.

And ne **gelæd** þu us **on** costnunge **ac** alys us **of** yfele.

Soþlice. (Luke 11:2-4)

[This page intentionally left blank]

# Chapter 5

# More Pronouns & Definite Article Rudiments

## 5.2 Vocabulary Exercises

### Translate the following phrases into Anglo-Saxon

1. so shine as the goldsmith's craft — scinan swa the goldsmið's cræft
2. thither the dimness of winter — Þider the dimnes of winter
3. the beans and eggs in the dish — the beans and ægs in the disc
4. Why the dog on the mat? — For-hwon the hund on the meatt?
5. red pepper — read pipor
6. how to heat the mead — hu hætan the meodu
7. to shove the shoulder of the short shepherd in the shire
   — scufan the sculdor/eaxl of the scort sceaphyrde in the scir
8. a good life and golden hearth — a god lif and gylden heorð
9. to defecate on the road — scitan on the road
10. judgment of the heathen — dom of the hæðen
11. the smell of peppercorn in the air — the stenc of piporcorn in the lyft
12. which fate of the witch — hywlc wyrd of the wicca
13. a net of shellfish — a nett of scilfisc
14. an inch of flesh and bone — an ince of flæsc and ban
15. fleece on the dock — flies on the docce
16. the leaf on the clay boat — the leaf on the clæg bat
17. a nation of Christian neighbors — a folc of Cristen neahgeburs
18. a pillow made of wool — a bolster wullen
19. one trinity — an ðrines
20. heavenly ribs — heofonlic ribs

## 5.4 Grammar Exercises

### Complete the charts for the following paradigms.

| | Masculine & Feminine |
|---|---|
| **Nominative** | hwa |
| **Genetive** | hwæs |
| **Dative** | hwæm |
| **Accusative** | hwone |

| | Neuter |
|---|---|
| **Nominative** | hwæt |
| **Genetive** | hwæs |
| **Dative** | hwæm |
| **Accusative** | hwæt |
| **Instrumental** | hwi |

| | Masculine | Feminine | Neuter |
|---|---|---|---|
| **Nominative** | þes | þeos | þis |
| **Genetive** | þisses | þisse | þisses |
| **Dative** | þissum | þisse | þissum |
| **Accusative** | þisne | þas | þis |
| Instrumental | þys | | þys |

| | Masculine, Feminine, & Neuter |
|---|---|
| **Nominative** | þas |
| **Genetive** | þissa |
| **Dative** | þissum |
| **Accusative** | þas |

| | Masculine | Feminine | Neuter |
|---|---|---|---|
| **Nominative** | se | seo | þæt |
| **Genetive** | þæs | þære | þæs |
| **Dative** | þæm | þære | þæm |
| **Accusative** | þone | þa | þæt |
| Instrumental | þy/þon | | þy/þon |

| | Masculine, Feminine, & Neuter |
|---|---|
| **Nominative** | þa |
| **Genetive** | þara |
| **Dative** | þæm |
| **Accusative** | þa |

## 5.5 Quiz

### Translate from Modern English into Anglo-Saxon (20 points)

1. whom (accusative) — hwone
2. to what (dative) — hwæm
3. who — hwa
4. whose — hwæs
5. what's — hwæs
6. to whom (dative) — hwæm
7. to this (dative, masculine) — þissum
8. with that (neuter) — þæm
9. those (feminine) — þa
10. the (neuter plural) — þa

### Translate from Anglo-Saxon to Modern English (1 point each)

11. hæþ — heather
12. flæsc — flesh
13. hætan — to heat
14. meodu — mead
15. ban — bone
16. hlid — lid
17. pipor — pepper
18. inc — inch
19. an — one
20. scilfisc — shellfish
21. wyrd — fate
22. lyft— air
23. folc— nation
24. docce — dock
25. rudu — red coloring
26. piporcorn — peppercorn
27. ðrines — trinity
28. cynn — kin
29. windeltreow — willow
30. sceaphyrde — shepherd
31. nædl — needle
32. hæsel — hazel
33. eald — old
34. hete — hatred
35. æl — eel

### Translate from Modern English to Anglo-Saxon (1 point each)

36. dog — hund
37. heavenly — heofonlic
38. neighbor — neahgebur
39. to shine — scinan
40. boat — bat
41. Christian — Cristen

## Translate from Modern English to Anglo-Saxon (continued)

42. judgment — dom
43. shoulder — sculdor, eaxl
44. goldsmith — goldsmið
45. sexual pleasure — wynlust
46. smell — stenc
47. pillow — bolster
48. shire — scir
49. brisk — snell
50. to make fast — fæstan
51. to become drunk — oferdrencan
52. shilling — scilling
53. heathen — hæðen
54. fleece — flies
55. egg — æg
56. pig — swin
57. flood — flod
58. beauty — glæm
59. peony — peonie
60. navel — nafela

## Fill in the blanks (30 points)

61.

**Fæder ure** þu þe **eart** on **heofonum**, si **þin** name **gehalgod** .

To **becume** þin **rice**, **gewurþe** ðin **willa** , on **eorðan** swa on **heofonum**.

Urne **gedæghwamlican** hlaf **syle** us **todæg**,

And **forgyf** us **ure gyltas swa swa** we **forgyfað** urum **gyltendum**.

And ne **gelæd** þu **us on** costnunge **ac alys** us **of yfele**.

**Soþlice**. (Luke 11:2-4)

# Chapter 6

# Adjective Rudiments

## 6.2 Vocabulary Exercises

### Translate the following phrases into Anglo-Saxon

1. to float on the plank — fleotan on the bord
2. eight heavy books — eahta hefig bocs
3. a door in the cliff — a duru in the clif
4. while the clean foal — hwil the clæne fola
5. meeting day in the orchard — meting in the ortgeard
6. thus the nether chair — Þus the neðera stol
7. that shrew and the effeminate man — that screwa and the bæddel
8. thanks to the shovel — ðonc to the scofl
9. ten thanes at the solid gold shrine — tien ðegns at the eallgylden scrin
10. the weasel and the vixen's wedding — the weosule and the fyxe's weddung
11. such are fell Vandals — Þyslic are fyllan Wendles
12. creator of goodness — metod of godnes
13. Where is the maker of yellow ale? — Hwær is the smið of geolu ealoð?
14. to undo the hedge — undon the hege
15. to shrink from the goose on the floor — scrincan from the gos on the flor
16. to melt away in the light — gemeltan in the liht
17. with help from kindred — with help from cynn
18. foam on the smith's beard — fam on the smið's beard
19. the way of the weather — the weg of the weder
20. to entrap the walker in darkness — betræppan the sceadu-genga

## 6.4 Grammar Exercises

### Exercise A

Fill in these weak adjectival endings.

**Singular**

| | Masculine | Feminine | Neuter |
|---|---|---|---|
| **Nominative** | se swifta | seo swifte | þæt swifte |
| **Genetive** | þæs swiftan | þære swiftan | þæs swiftan |
| **Dative** | þæm swiftan | þære swiftan | þæm swiftan |
| **Accusative** | þone swiftan | þa swiftan | þæt swifte |

**Plural**

| | Masculine, Feminine, & Neuter |
|---|---|
| **Nominative** | þa swiftan |
| **Genetive** | þara swiftena /swiftra |
| **Dative** | þæm swiftum |
| **Accusative** | þa swiftan |

### Exercise B

Fill in these strong adjectival endings.

**Singular**

| | Masculine | Feminine | Neuter |
|---|---|---|---|
| **Nominative** | swift | swift | swift |
| **Genetive** | swiftes | swiftre | swiftes |
| **Dative** | swiftum | swiftre | swiftum |
| **Accusative** | swiftne | swifte | swift |
| **Instrmental** | swifte | | swifte |

**Plural**

| | Masculine | Feminine | Neuter |
|---|---|---|---|
| **Nominative** | swifte | swifta | swift |
| **Genetive** | swiftra | swiftra | swiftra |
| **Dative** | swiftum | swiftum | swiftum |
| **Accusative** | swifte | swifta | swift |

## Exericse C

### Write "swifter than I" in Anglo-Saxon.

**swiftra ðonne ic**

### Give the positive, comparative, and superlative forms for the following adjectives:

| | Positive | Comparative | Superlative |
|---|---|---|---|
| **young** | geong | gingra | gingest |
| **long** | lang | lengra | longest |
| **good** | god | betera | betst |
| **bad** | yfel | wiersa | wierst |

## 6.5 Quiz

### Complete the sentences by filling in the blanks (27 points).

Use the best Anglo-Saxon version of *se swifta guma, seo swifte hand*, or *þæt swifte scip*. Pay attention to your case endings. Some of the answers may be either singular or plural.

1. I saw [þæt swifte scip] as it came towards the cliff.
2. [ Seo swifte hand] was clenched in a fist.
3. They placed the laurels on the head of [þæs swiftan guman].
4. With the sword in [þære swoftam handa], the battle is won.
5. There were over one hundred sailors divided among [þæm swiftum scipum] .
6. The Vikings were [þa swiftan guman] who raided the coast.
7. [Þæt swifte scip] rides the waves.
8. The giant ring flashed with the movement of [þære swiftan handa].
9. They fed [þa swiftan guman] after their hard battle.

### Translate from Anglo-Saxon to Modern English (1 point each).

10. ðegn — thane
11. smið — smith/maker
12. weosule — weasel
13. geolu — yellow
14. ðonc — thanks
15. Wendle — Vandle
16. turf — sod
17. dæd — feat
18. siðian — travel
19. scofl — shovel
20. stan — stone
21. soð(lic) — true
22. flyht — flight
23. metod — creator
24. liht — light
25. foddor — fodder
26. eallgylden — solid gold
27. meting — meeting day
28. ortgeard — orchard
29. fleotan — to float
30. strand — beach, riverbank
31. eorðtilð — agriculture
32. stingan — to pierce
33. hord — treasure
34. sceað — sheath

## Translate from Modern English to Anglo-Saxon (1 point each).

35. eight — eahta
36. heavy — hefig
37. book — boc
38. chair — stol
39. web — webb
40. shower — scur
41. goodness — godnes
42. down — dun
43. cleanness — clænnes
44. word — word
45. nether — neðera
46. weather — weder
47. to undo — undon
48. to entrap — betræppan
49. ale — ealoð
50. to shrink — scrincan
51. to melt away — gemeltan
52. way — weg
53. pin — pinn
54. kindred — cynn
55. sky — heofan
56. trinity — ðrines
57. short — scort
58. fate — wyrd
59. shell — sciell

Fill in the blanks (23 points, ½ point for each blank):

60.

Fæder **ure þu þe eart** on **heofonum**, si **þin name gehalgod** .
To **becume þin rice, gewurþe ðin willa , on eorðan swa on heofonum.**
Urne **gedæghwamlican hlaf syle us todæg,**
And **forgyf us ure gyltas swa swa we forgyfað urum gyltendum.**
And **ne gelæd þu us on costnunge ac alys us of yfele.**
**Soþlice.** (Luke 11:2-4)

[This page intentionally left blank]

# Chapter 7
# Adverb Rudiments

## 7.2 Vocabulary Exercises

### Translate from Modern English into Anglo-Saxon.

1. God's wrist — God's wrist
2. the belt and broth of a deaf elder — the belt and broth of a deaf ealdor
3. to forget the gospel — forgietan the godspel
4. the marvel of Christmas Eve — the wundor of Modraniht
5. the warder of hellish spirits — the ræplingweard of hellegasts
6. the pleasure of asparagus in soup — the lust of eorðnafola in broð
7. never to untie the werewolf — næfre untigan the werwulf
8. a field of plants — a æcer of wyrts
9. when to fill the wharf — hwonne fyllan the hwearf
10. Welcome, child! — Wilcume, bearn!
11. the wet weevil in the wellspring — the wæt wifel in the wyllsprynge
12. the tug of quiet desire — dragan like stille lust
13. soon the silver organ — sona the seolfor organa
14. the sinful folk in hell — the synful folc in hel
15. to climb with the king — climban with the cyng
16. foot in the nettle — fot in the netle
17. the piper at midnight — the pipere at middenniht
18. the silversmith's thin sister — the seolforsmið's ðynne sweostor
19. to become hard like a solid iron thing — hyrdan like an ealliren ðing
20. yes, an apple in the grass — giese, an æppel in the gærs

## 7.4 Grammar Exercises

### Exercise A - What are the six possible endings for Anglo-Saxon adverbs?

| | | | | | |
|---|---|---|---|---|---|
| *— e* | *— lice* | *— inga* | *— um* | *— es* | *— a* |

### Exercise B - Translate into Anglo-Saxon.

1. angrily — wraþe
2. deeply — deope
3. truly — soðlice
4. recently — niwinga
5. fiercely — grame
6. painfully — sarlice
7. keenly — cene
8. more keenly — cenor
9. most keenly — cenost
10. poorly — earme
11. more poorly — earmor
12. most poorly — earmost
13. well — wel
14. better — bet
15. best — betst
16. little — lyt
17. less — læs
18. least — læst

## 7.5 Quiz

### Translate from Modern English into Anglo-Saxon (1 point each):

1. painfully — sarlice
2. more recently — niwingor
3. most truly — soðlicost
4. angrily — wraþe
5. deeply — deope
6. most fiercely — gramost
7. more deeply — deopor
8. most angrily — wraþost
9. truly — soðlice
10. recently — niwinga

## Create adverbs out of these Anglo-Saxon adjectives then translate each adverb into Modern English (50 points)

There will be options, so yours might not match those in the answer key.

11. blind — blinde / blindly
12. cymlic — cymlica / beautifully
13. mirce — mircelice / darkly
14. dimm — dimmes / dimly
15. deoflic — deoflice / devishly
16. great — greatum / largely
17. sealt — sealta / saltily
18. gylden — gyldenes / goldenly
19. yfel — yfellice / evilly
20. fæger — fægeringa / fairly
21. clæne — clæne / cleanly
22. freo — freolice / freely
23. wordig — wordiges / verbosely
24. hefig — hefiges / heavily
25. snell — snelle / briskly
26. glæd — glæde / gladly
27. isig — isiges / icily
28. sinful — sinfule / sinfully
29. wearm — wearminga / warmly
30. wær — wærlice / warily
31. tam — tames / tamely
32. horsc — horsclice / harshly
33. snotor — snotoringa / cleverly
34. biter — biteres / bitterly
35. unmihtig — unmihtigum / weakly

## Translate from Anglo-Saxon into Modern English (20 points)

36. climban — to climb
37. middenniht — midnight
38. broð — soup
39. hel — hell
40. middæg — midday
41. forgietan — to forget
42. wyllsprynge — wellspring
43. næfre — never
44. breost — breast
45. bearn — child
46. werwulf — werewolf
47. dragan — to tug
48. hwearf — wharf
49. middeweard — in the middle
50. ðawian — to thaw
51. neðera — nether
52. cynn — family, kin, kindred
53. godnes — goodness
54. clænnes — cleanness
55. beard — beard

## Translate from Modern English into Anglo-Saxon (20 points)

56. gospel — godspel
57. belt — belt
58. king — cyng
59. hellish spirit — hellegast
60. ridge — hrycg
61. silversmith — seolforsmið
62. welcome! — wilcume
63. sin — synn, gylt
64. yes — giese
65. marvel — wundor
66. solid iron — ealliren
67. warder — ræplingweard
68. asparagus — eorðnafola
69. pleasure — lust
70. Christmas Eve — Modraniht
71. maker — smið
72. chair — stol
73. yellow — geolu
74. to undo — undon
75. foal — fola

## Write out The Lord's Prayer from memory

You should know the Lord's Prayer by now. (0 points, but it'll be worth more on the final exam)

76.

**Fæder ure þu þe eart on heofonum, si þin name gehalgod .**
**To becume þin rice, gewurþe ðin willa , on eorðan swa on heofonum.**
**Urne gedæghwamlican hlaf syle us todæg,**
**And forgyf us ure gyltas swa swa we forgyfað urum gyltendum.**
**And ne gelæd þu us on costnunge ac alys us of yfele.**
**Soþlice. (Luke 11:2-4)**

# Chapter 8

# Unit One - Final Exam 200 points

The following exam is taken from the quizzes at the ends of chapters 1-7, so if you review the quizzes, you'll do fine. The only exception is the vocabulary section, which draws from the comprehensive lists that open the chapters. In other words, you'll need to study all the vocab, not just the words that showed up on the quizzes.

## 8.1 Verbs

### Complete the chart for the following verbs (10 points)

| | **standan** |
|---|---|
| Infinitive | standan |
| First | stande |
| Second | stentst |
| Third | stent |
| Plural | standaþ |

| | **feohtan** |
|---|---|
| Infinitive | feohtan |
| First | feohte |
| Second | fiehtst |
| Third | fieht |
| Plural | feohtaþ |

## 8.2 Nouns

### Fill out the appropriate endings (16 points)

| | **Singular** | **Plural** |
|---|---|---|
| **Nominative** | nama | naman |
| **Genetive** | naman | namena |
| **Dative** | naman | namum |
| **Accusative** | naman | naman |

### Fill out the appropriate endings (16 points)

| | Singular | Plural |
|---|---|---|
| Nominative | hand | handa |
| Genetive | handa | handa |
| Dative | handa | handum |
| Accusative | hand | handa |

### Complete the sentences by filling in the blanks with the best Anglo-Saxon option (3 points)

1. The dragon lay curled on top of its great pile of [ welan ].
2. Helen of Troy launched a thousand [ scipu ].
3. The [ naman ] of the warriors were Beowulf and Wiglaf.

## 8.3 Pronouns

### Translate the following (14 points)

1. ge — you all
2. hie — they
3. ic — I
4. hira — theirs
5. eowic — you
6. he — he
7. heo — she

8. He follows. — He folgaþ.
9. You all come. — Ge cumaþ.
10. We ride. — We ridaþ.
11. They stand. — Hie standaþ.
12. You rode. — You ride.
13. We stand. — We standaþ.
14. It fights. — Hit fieht.

### Fill in the following chart (13 points)

| | Masculine | Feminine | Neuter |
|---|---|---|---|
| Nominative | þes | þeos | þis |
| Genetive | þisses | þisse | þisses |
| Dative | þissum | þisse | þissum |
| Accusative | þisne | þas | þis |
| Instrumental | þys | | þys |

## 8.4 Adjectives

### Fill in these strong adjectival endings (26 points):

Singular

| | Masculine | Feminine | Neuter |
|---|---|---|---|
| **Nominative** | swift | swift | swift |
| **Genetive** | swiftes | swiftre | swiftes |
| **Dative** | swiftum | swiftre | swiftum |
| **Accusative** | swiftne | swifte | swift |
| **Instrmental** | swifte | | swifte |

Plural

| | Masculine | Feminine | Neuter |
|---|---|---|---|
| **Nominative** | swifte | swifta | swift |
| **Genetive** | swiftra | swiftra | swiftra |
| **Dative** | swiftum | swiftum | swiftum |
| **Accusative** | swifte | swifta | swift |

### Complete the sentences (9 Points)

Fill in the blanks with the best Anglo-Saxon version of *se swifta guma*, *seo swifte hand*, or *Þæt swifte scip*. Some of the answers may be either singular or plural (9 points):

1. I saw [ **þæt swifte scip** ] as it came towards the cliff.

2. They placed the laurels on the head of [ **þæs swiftan guman** ].

3. The giant ring flashed with the movement of [ **þære swiftan handa** ].

## 8.5 Adverbs

### Create adverbs out of these Anglo-Saxon adjectives, then translate each adverb into Modern English (10 points, answers may vary)

1. gylden — glydenes / goldenly
2. wordig — wordigum / verbosely
3. horsc — horsclice / harshly
4. snotor — snotoringa / cleverly
5. freo — freolice / freely

## 8.6 Vocabulary

### Translate from Anglo-Saxon into Modern English, or Modern English into Anglo-Saxon (50 points)

1. ancient duty — ealdriht
2. wæterfæsten — camp protected by water
3. bastard — bastard
4. middangeard — world, earth
5. just as — swa swa
6. ðegn — thane
7. baby — bearn, cradolcild
8. gemeltan — to melt away
9. haven — hæfen
10. fæderlic — fatherly
11. devil — deofol
12. merscmealuwe — marshmallow
13. marsh — mersc
14. aweccan — to awaken
15. air — lyft
16. deaðwic — abode of the dead
17. paradise — paradis
18. snotor — clever
19. historian — wyrdwritere
20. scyrpan — to sharpen
21. sandy beach — sondland
22. wudefæsten — camp protected by wood
23. accident — belimp
24. yfelnes — wickedness
25. jail — carcern
26. bealoful — deadly
27. satisfaction — bliss
28. earwicga — earwig
29. baptism — fulluht
30. Haligdæg — Sunday
31. mankind — moncynn
32. wæpn — weapon
33. treasure — hord
34. twiseltoþ — bucktoothed
35. fate — wyrd
36. stingan — to pierce
37. seawall — sæweall
38. Easterdæg — Easter Sunday
39. willow — windeltreow
40. mynstermonn — monk
41. to shine — scinan
42. sceaphyrde — shepherd
43. seven — seofon
44. oferdrencan — to become drunk
45. solid gold — eallgylden
46. Þrines — Trinity
47. gospel — godspel
48. betræppan — to entrap
49. effeminate man — bæddel
50. hellegast — hellish spirit

## 8.7 Memorization

### Write out the Lord's Prayer in Anglo-Saxon (49 points)

**Fæder ure þu þe eart on heofonum, si þin name gehalgod .**

**To becume þin rice, gewurþe ðin willa , on eorðan swa on heofonum.**

**Urne gedæghwamlican hlaf syle us todæg,**

**And forgyf us ure gyltas swa swa we forgyfað urum gyltendum.**

**And ne gelæd þu us on costnunge ac alys us of yfele.**

**Soþlice. (Luke 11:2-4)**

[This page intentionally left blank]

UNIT TWO

# TRANSLATION RUDIMENTS

[This page intentionally left blank]

# Chapter 9

# Translation (Part 1)

### Mark 1:1-13, Mark 2:1-12, Mark 4:1-20

## 9.2 Vocabulary Exercises

### Translate the following phrases/sentences into Anglo-Saxon

1. to drag the empty horn — dragan the æmtig horn
2. blind swan in the broad nest — blind swan in the brad nest
3. to forswear greatness — forswerian greatnes
4. a herd of herring — a heord of hæring
5. to vomit the vegetables next — spiwan the wyrts æftera
6. to sit in the night — sittan in the niht
7. the right hand of the mighty organist — the rihthand of the mihtig organestre
8. the king's daughter with a lisp — the cwen with a wlips
9. Hey! A parable! — Hig! / Hwæt! A bigspell!
10. which of two sledgehammers — which of two slecgs
11. to smear the wheel with cider — smerian the hweohl with æppelwin
12. however the pledge — hwæder the wedd
13. the hide of the Irish whelp — the hyd of the Irisc hwelp
14. to spend the winter in a decorated church — oferwintrian in a fag cirice
15. The member of a guild is alive. — The gegilda is cwic.
16. to slide nigh the pit — slidan neah the pytt / hol
17. Here is the greedy bedfellow. — Her is the grædig gebedda.
18. sleep in midsummer — slæp / ræst in middansumer
19. nevertheless six new plums — hwæðer siex niw plymes
20. the third slow smithy — the ðridda slaw smiððe

## 9.3 Translation—Mark 1:1-13

1. Her ys godspelles angyn Hælendes Cristes, Godes suna;
[Here is the beginning of the gospel of Savior, Christ, the Son of God;]

2. Swa awriten is on ðæs witegan bec Isaiam, Nu! ic asende minne engel beforan ðinre ansyne, se gegearwaþ ðinne weg beforan ðe
[As it is written in the book of the prophet Isaiah, Behold, I send my messenger before thy face, which shall prepare thy way before thee]

3. Clypigende stefen on ðam westene, Gegearwiaþ Drihtnes weg, doþ rihte his siðas
[The voice of one crying in the wilderness, Prepare ye the way of the Lord, make his paths straight]

4. Iohannes wæs on westene fulligende, and bodiende dæd-bote fulwiht, on synna forgyfenesse
[John was in the wilderness baptizing and preaching the baptism of repentance for the remission of sins]

5. And to him ferde eall Iudeisc rice, and ealle Hierosolima-ware; and wæron fram him gefullode on Iordanes flode, hyra synna anddetende
[And there went out unto him all the land of Judaea, and they of Jerusalem, and were all baptized of him in the river of Jordan, confessing their sins]

6. And Iohannes wæs gescryd mid oluendes hærum, and fellen gyrdel wæs ymbe his lendenu; and gærstapan, and wudu hunig he æt;
[And John was clothed with camel's hair, and with a girdle of a skin about his loins; and he did eat locusts and wild honey;]

7. And he bodode, and cwæþ, Strengra cymþ æfter me, ðæs ne eom ic wyrðe ðæt ic his sceona þwanga bugende uncnytte
[And preached, saying, There cometh one mightier after me, the latchet of whose shoes I am not worthy to stoop down and unloose]

8. Ic fullige eow on wætere; he eow fullaþ on Halgum Gaste.
[I baptize you in water: but he shall baptize you in the Holy Ghost.]

9. And on ðam dagum, come se Hælend fram Nazareth Galilee, and wæs gefullod on Iordane fram Iohanne.
[And in those days, the Savior came from Nazareth of Galilee, and was baptized of John in Jordan.]

10. And sona of ðam wætere, he geseah opene heofonas, and Haligne Gast swa culfran astigende, and on him wunigende:
[And straightway coming up out of the water, he saw the heavens opened, and the Holy Spirit like a dove descending and remaining upon him:]

11. And ða wæs stefn of heofenum geworden, Ðu eart min gelufoda suna, on ðe ic gelicode
[And there came a voice from heaven, Thou art my beloved Son, in whom I am well pleased.]

12. And sona Gast hine on westen genydde.
[And immediately the Spirit driveth him into the wilderness. ]

13. And he on westene wæs feowertig daga and feowertig nihta, and he wæs fram Satane gecostnod, and he mid wilddeorum wæs, and him englas þenodon.
[And he was in the wilderness forty days and forty nights, and he was tempted of Satan; and was with the wild beasts; and the angels ministered unto him.]

## 9.4 TRANSLATION [MARK 2:1-12]

1. And eft æfter dagum, he eode into Cafarnaum. And hit wæs gehyred, ðæt he wæs on huse,
[And again he entered into Capernaum after some days; and it was heard that he was in the house.]

2. And manega togædere comon, . . . And he to heom spræc.
[And many came together, . . . And he spoke to them.]

3. And hi comon anne laman to him berende, ðone feower men bæron.
[And they come unto him, bringing one lame whom for men carried.]

4. And ða hi ne mihton hine in-bringan for ðære mænigeo, hi openodon ðone hrof, ðar se Hælend wæs; and ... hi ða in-asendon ðæt bed, ðe se lama on-læg.
[And when they could not bring him in on account of the crowd, they opened the roof where the Savior was: and ... they let down the bed in which the lame man lay.]

5. Soþlice ða se Hælend geseah heora geleafan, he cwæþ to ðam laman, Sunu, ðe synt ðine synna forgifene.
[When the Savior saw their faith, he said unto the lame man, Son, thy sins be forgiven thee.]

6. Ðar wæron sume of ðam bocerum sittende, and on heora heortan þencende,
[Some of the scribes were sitting there, and reasoning in their hearts,]

7. Hwi spycþ ðes ðus? He dysegaþ; hwa mæg synna forgyfan, buton God ana?
[Why speaks this man thus? Who can forgive sins but God only?]

8. Ða se Hælend ðæt on his gaste oncneow, ðæt hi swa betwux him þohton, he cweaþ to him, Hwi þence ge ðas þing on eowrum heortum?
[When the Savior perceived in his spirit that they so reasoned within themselves, he said unto them, Why reason ye these things in your hearts?]

9. Hwæðer is eðre to secgenne to ðam laman, Ðe synd ðine synna forgifene, hwæðer ðe cweðan, Aris, nim ðin bed, and ga?
[Whether is it easier to say to the lame man, Thy sins be forgiven thee; or to say, Arise, and take up thy bed, and walk?]

10. Ðæt ge soþlice witon ðæt mannes sunu hæfþ anweald on eorþan synna to forgyfanne, he cwæþ to ðam laman,
[That ye may truly know that the Son of man hath power on earth to forgive sins, (he saith to the lame man,)]

11. Ðe ic secge, aris, nim ðin bed, and ga to ðinum huse,
[I say unto thee, Arise, take up thy bed, and go into thine house.]

12. And he sona aras, and, underleat bere, beforan him eallum eode, swa ðæt ealle wundredon, … and ðus cwædon, Næfre we ær ðyllic ne gesawon.
[And immediately he arose, took up the bed, and went forth before them all; insomuch that they all marvelled ... and spoke thus, We never saw it on this fashion.]

## 9.5 TRANSLATION [MARK 4:1-20]

1. And eft he ongan hi æt ðære sæ læran; and him wæs mycel menegu to gegaderod, swa ðæt he on scip eode, and on ðære sæ wæs, and eall seo menegu ymbe ða sæ wæs, on lande.
[And he began again to teach them by the sea side: and there was gathered unto him a great multitude, so that he entered into a ship, and was on the sea; and the whole multitude was by the sea on the land.]

2. And he hi fela on bigspellum lærde. And him to cwæþ on hys lare,
[And he taught them many things by parables, and said unto them in his doctrine,]

3. Gehyraþ. Ut eode se sædere his sæd to sawenne.
[Hearken; The Sower, there went out to sow:]

4. And ða he sew, sum feoll wið ðone weg, and fugelas comon, and hit fræton.
[And when as he sowed, some fell by the way side, and fowls came and devoured it up.]

5. Sum feoll ofer stan-scyligean, ðar hit næfde mycele eorþan; and sona upeode, forðam ðe hit næfde eorþan þiccnesse.
[Some fell on stony ground, where it had not much earth; and immediately it sprang up, because it had no depth of earth:]

6. Ða hit up-eode, seo sunne hit forswælde, and hit forscranc, forðam hit wyrtruman næfde.
[When it came up, the sun scorched it, and it withered, because it had no root.]

7. And sum feoll on þornas, ða stigon ða þornas, and forþrysmodon ðæt, and hit wæstm ne bær.
[And some fell among thorns, then the thorns grew up, and choked it, and it yielded no fruit.]

8. And sum feoll on god land, and hit sealde, uppstigende, and wexende, wæstm; and an brohte þritig-fealdne, sum syxtigfealdne, sum hund-fealdne.
[And other fell on good ground, and did yield fruit, springing up and growing; and some brought forth, thirty-fold, and some sixty, and some an hundred.]

9. And he cwæþ, Gehyre, se ðe earan hæbbe to gehyranne.
[And he said, He that hath ears to hear, let him hear.]

10. And ða he ana wæs, hine axodon ðæt bigspell ða twelfe ðe mid him wæron.
[And when he was alone, the twelve who were with him asked of him the parable.]

11. And he sæde him, Eow is geseald to witanne Godes rices gerynu. Ðam ðe ute synd, ealle þing on bigspellum gewurðaþ.
[And he said unto them, Unto you it is given to know the mysteries of the kingdom of God: unto them that are without, all these things are done in parables:]

12. Ðæt hi geseonde geseon, and na ne geseon, and gehyrende gehyron, and ne ongyton; ðe-læs hi hwænne syn gecyrede, and him sin hyra synna forgyfene.
[That seeing they may see, and not perceive; and hearing they may hear, and not understand; lest at any time they should be converted, and their sins should be forgiven them.]

## 9.5 TRANSLATION [MARK 4:1-20] Continued

13. Ða sæde he him, Ge nyton ðis bigspell and hu mage ge ealle bigspell witan?
[Then he said unto them, Know ye not this parable? and how then will ye all know parables?]

14. Se ðe sæwþ, word he sæwþ.
[He who sows, soweth the word.]

15. Soþlice ða synd wið ðone weg, ðar ðæt word is gesawen; and ðonne hi hit gehyraþ, sona cymþ Satanas, and afyrþ ðæt word ðe on heora heortan asawen ys.
[Truly they are by the way side, where the word is sown; and when they hear it, Satan cometh immediately, and taketh away the word that was sown in their hearts.]

16. And ða synd gelice ðe synd ofer ða stan-scylian gesawen, sona ðænne hi ðæt word gehyraþ, and ðæt mid blisse onfoþ;
[And they are likewise which are sown on stony ground; as soon as they hear the word, and immediately receive it with gladness;]

17. And hi nabbaþ wyrtruman on him, ac beoþ unsaðolfæste; and syððan upcymþ deofles costnung, and his ehtnys for ðam worde….
[And have no root in themselves, but are unsteadfast: afterward, when the devil's temptation ariseth, and his persecution for the word....]

18. Hi synd on þornum gesawen ðæt synd; ða ðe þæt word gehyraþ,
[These are they which are sown among thorns; such as hear the word,]

19. And of yrmþe, and swicdome worold-welena, and oðra gewilnunga, ðæt word of-þrysmiaþ, and synd buton wæstme gewordene.
[And the cares of this world, and the deceitfulness of riches, and the lusts of other things entering in, choke the word, and they became unfruitful.]

20. And ða ðe gesawene synd ofer ðæt gode land, ða synd ðe ðæt word gehyraþ, and onfoþ, and wæstm bringaþ, sum þritig-fealdne, sum syxtig-fealdne, and sum hund-fealdne.
[And they who are sown on good ground; they are the ones who hear the word, and receive it, and bring forth fruit, some thirtyfold, some sixty, and some an hundred.]

## 9.6 Quiz

### Translate from Anglo-Saxon into Modern English (25 points)

1. fag — decorated
2. wedd — pledge
3. horn — horn
4. æppelwin — cidar
5. oferwintrian — to spend the winter
6. cwen — king's wife or daughter
7. grædig — greedy
8. spiwan — to vomit
9. siextiene — sixteen
10. slæpan — to sleep
11. dumb — dumb
12. smiððe — smithy
13. dragan — to drag
14. brad — broad
15. forca — fork
16. middansumer — midsummer
17. hæring — herring
18. wlips — lisp
19. forswerian — to forswear
20. rihthand — right hand
21. hol — pit
22. neah — nigh
23. gegilda — member of a guild
24. hweohl — wheel
25. mot — speck

### Translate from Modern English into Ango-Saxon (25 points)

26. parable — bigspell
27. empty — æmtig
28. device — orðanc
29. new — niw
30. to thirst — ðyrstan
31. companion — gesið
32. here — her
33. upper story — upflor
34. organist — organestre
35. hey! — hig! / hwæt!
36. alive — cwic
37. sledgehammer — slecg
38. Irish — Irisc
39. helmet — helm
40. bedfellow — gebedda
41. church — cirice
42. slow — slaw
43. linseed — linsæd
44. pole — post / pal
45. vegetable — wyrt
46. decorated — fag
47. to slide — slidan
48. plum — plyme
49. night — niht
50. midway — midd

## Fill in the blanks (50 points)

51.

**Hwaet**! We Gar-Đena in geardagum,
þeodcyninga, þrym **gefrunon**,
hu ða **æþelingas** ellen fremedon.
Oft Scyld **Scefing** sceaþena þreatum,
monegum mægþum, meodosetla **ofteah**,
egsode eorlas. **Syððan** ærest wearð
feasceaft **funden**, he þæs frofre gebad,
weox under **wolcnum**, weorðmyndum þah,
oð þæt him **æghwylc** þara ymbsittendra
ofer hronrade hyran scolde,
gomban gyldan. Þæt wæs god **cyning**!

[This page intentionally left blank]

# Chapter 10

# Translation (Part 2)

## Mark 5:1-15, Mark 5:16-30, Mark 5:31-43

### 10.2 Vocabulary Exercises

#### Translate the following phrases/sentences from Modern English into Anglo-Saxon:

1. a drink from the foul brook — a drenc from the ful broc
2. thirty Irishmen upon the high seas — ðritig Scottas uppan the heahsæ
3. Whither the sore beetle? — Hwider the sar ceafer?
4. law of the ancestor — riht of the ealdfæder
5. to wield a fishhook — wieldan an angil
6. clutch of a filthy claw — grap of an unclæne clea
7. the stillborn's spirit — the deadboren's gast
8. wide wood for a house — wid boldtimber
9. a pot of stew — a crocca of broð
10. nightlong snow — nihtlong snaw
11. to miss by a mile — missan by a mil
12. four green kirtles — feower grene cyrtele
13. hither on the turf — hider on the turf
14. little bolster made of linen — lytel bolster linen
15. rime on the nightclothes — hrim on the nihtwaru
16. snake in the smooth pool — snaca / wyrm in the smoð wæl
17. whistling son of a widow — hwistlung sunu of a widewe
18. whore in the Bible — hore in the biblioðece
19. distant constellations — feorr tungols
20. a snail in the thistle — a snægl in the ðistel

## 10.3 Translation—Mark 5:1-15

1 Ða comon hi ofer ðære sæs muþan on ðæt rice Hierasenorum.

[And they came over the mouth of the sea, into the country of the Gadarenes.]

2 And hym of scipe gangendum, him sona agen arn an man of dam byrgenum on unclænum gaste.

[And as he was going out of the ship, immediately there met him out of the tombs a man with an unclean spirit,]

3 Se hæfde on byrgenum scræf, and hine nan man mid racenteagum ne mihte gebindan.

[Who had his dwelling among the tombs; and no man could bind him with chains:]

4 Forðam he oft mid fot-copsum and racenteagum gebunden, toslat ða raceteaga, and ða fot-copsas tobræc, and hine nan man gewyldan ne mihte.

[For often, bound with fetters and chains, he broke the chains and smashed the fetters, and no man could tame him.]

5 And symle, dæges and nihtes, he wæs on byrgenum and on muntum, hrymende, and hine sylfne mid stanum ceorfende.

[And always, night and day, he was in the mountains, and in the tombs, crying, and cutting himself with stones.]

6 Soþlice ða he ðone Hæland feorran geseah, he arn, and hine gebæd.

[When he saw the Savior afar off, he ran and worshipped him,]

7 And mycelre stemne hrymende, and ðus cwæþ, Eala mæra Hælend, Godes sunu, hwæt is me and ðe? Ic halsige ðe þurh God, ðæt ðu me ne þreage.

[And crying with a loud voice, he spoke thus, O great Savior, Son of God, What have I to do with thee? I adjure thee by God, that thou torment me not.]

8Ða cwæþ se Hælend, Eala unclæna gast, ga of ðysum men.

[Then the Savior said unto him, O thou unclean spirit, go out of this man.]

9 Ða ahsode he hyne, Hwæt is ðin nama? Ða cwæþ he, Min nama is legio; forðam we manega synd.

[Then he asked him, What is thy name? Then he said, My name is Legion: for we are many.]

10 And he hine swyðe bæd, ðæt he hine of ðam rice ne nydde.

[And he besought him much that he would not send them away out of the country.]

11 Ðar wæs embe ðone munt mycel swyna heord læswigende.

[There was nigh unto that mountain a great herd of swine feeding.]

12 And ða unclænan gastas hyne bædon, and cwædon, Send us on ðas swyn, ðæt we on hi gegan.

[And the unclean spirits besought him and said, Send us into the swine, that we may enter into them.]

13 And ða lyfde se Hælend sona. And ða eodon ða unclænan gastas on ða swyn, and on myclum hryre seo heord wearþ on sæ bescofen, twa þusendo, and wurdon adruncene on ðære sæ.

[And forthwith Jesus gave them leave. And then the unclean spirits went into the swine, and with a great fall the herd was thrown into the sea, two thousand, and were choked in the sea.]

14 Soþlice ða ðe hi heoldon, flugon, and cyðdon on ðære ceastre, and on lande; and hi uteodon, ðæt hi gesawon hwæt ðar gedon wære.

[Then those who kept them fled, and told it in the city, and in the country. And they went out that they might see what it was that was done there.]

15 And hi comon to ðam Hælende, and hi gesawon ðone ðe mid deofle gedreht wæs, gescrydne sittan, and hales modes; and hi him ondredon.

[And they came to the Savior, and saw him that was possessed with the devil, and had the legion, clothed, sitting, and of whole mind: and they feared him.]

## 10.4 Translation—Mark 5:16-30

16 And hi rehton him, ða ðe hit gesawon, hu hit gedon wæs be ðam ðe deofol-seocnesse hæfde, and be ðam swynum.
[And they that saw it told them how it was done to him that had the devil-sickness and also concerning the swine.]

17 And hi bædon, ðæt he of hyra gemærum fore.
[And they bad him depart out of their lands.]

18 Ða he on scip eode, hine ongan biddan, se ðe ær mid deofle gedreht wæs, ðæt he mid him wære.
[When he was come into the ship, he that had been possessed with the devil began to pray that he might be with him.]

19 Him ða se Hælend ne getiðode, ac he sæde him, Ga to ðinum huse to ðinum hiwum, and cyþ him, hu mycel Drihten gedyde, and he gemiltsode ðe.
[Then the Savior suffered him not, but saith unto him, Go home to thy friends, and tell them how great things the Lord hath done, and hath had compassion on thee.]

20 And he ða ferde, and ongan bodigean on Decapolim, hu fela se Hælend him dyde; and hig ealle ðæs wundredon.
[And then he departed, and began to publish in Decapolis how great things Jesus had done for him: and they all marvelled at it.]

21 And ða se Hælend eft on scype ferde ofer ðone muþan, him com to mycel menigu, and wæs ymbe ða sæ.
[And when the Savior passed over the mouth by ship unto the other side, much people gathered unto him: and he was nigh unto the sea.]

22 And ða com sum of heah-gesamnungum, Iairus hatte, and ða he hyne geseah, he astrehte hine to his fotum,
[And then one of the rulers of the synagogue came, Jairus by name; and when he saw him, he fell at his feet,]

23 And hine swyðe bæd, and he cwæþ, Min dohtor is on ytemestum siðe; cum, and sete ðine hand ofer hi, ðæt heo hal sy, and lybbe.

[And besought him greatly, and he said, My daughter lieth at the point of death: come and lay thy hand on her, that she may be whole, and live.]

24 Ða ferde he mid him, and him fyligde mycel menigeo, and þrungon hine.

[Then he went with him; and much people followed him, and thronged him.]

25 And ða ðæt wif ðe on blodes ryne twelf winter wæs,

[And then it happened that a woman, which had an issue of blood twelve years,]

26 And fram manegum læcum fela þinga þolode, and dælde eall ðæt heo ahte, and hit naht ne fremode, ac wæs ðe wyrse.

[And suffered many things of many physicians, and spent all that she had, and it availed nothing, but was the worse,]

27 Ða heo be ðam Hælende gehyrde, heo com wið-æftan ða menigu, and his reaf æt-hran.

[When she heard about the Savior, she came after the crowd, and touched his garment.]

28 Soþlice heo cwæþ, Gif ic furðon his reafes æt-hrin, ic beo hal

[For she said, If I may touch but his clothes, I shall be whole.]

29 And ða sona wearþ hyre blodes ryne adruwod, and heo on hire gefredde ðæt heo of ðam wite gehæled wæs.

[And then straightway the fountain of her blood was dried up; and she felt in her body that she was healed of that plague.]

30 And ða se Hælend oncneow on him silfum ðæt him mægen of eode, he cwæþ, bewend to ðære menigu, Hwa æt-hran mines reafes?

[And then the Savior knew in himself that virtue had gone out of him, turned to the crowd, Who touched my clothes?]

## 10.5 Translation—Mark 5:31-43

31 Ða cwædon his leorning-cnihtas, Ðu gesyhst ðas menigu ðe þringende, and ðu cwyst, Hwa æt-hran me?

[And his disciples said, Thou seest the multitude thronging thee, and sayest thou, Who touched me?]

32 And ða beseah hine, ðæt he gesawe ðæne ðe ðæt dyde.

[And he looked round about to see her that had done it.]

33 Ðat wif ða ondrædende and forhtigende, … com, and astrehte hi beforan him, and sæde him eall ðæt riht.

[But the woman fearing and trembling, … came and fell down before him, and told him all the truth.]

34 Ða cwæþ se Hælend, Dohtor, ðin geleafa ðe hale gedyde; ga ðe on sibbe, and beo of ðisum hal.

[Thus the Savior said unto her, Daughter, thy faith hath made thee whole; go in peace, and be whole of this.]

35 Him ða gyt sprecendum, hi comon fram ðam heah-gesamnungum, and cwædon, Ðin dohtor is dead; hwi drecst ðu leng ðone lareow?

[While he yet spake, they came from the ruler of the synagogue's house certain which said, Thy daughter is dead: why troublest thou the teacher any further?]

36 Ða he gehyrde ðæt word, ða cwæþ se Hælend, Ne ondræd ðu ðe, gelyf for an.

[When he heard the word the Savior said, Be not afraid, only believe.]

37 And he ne let him ænig ne fyligean, buton Petrum, and Iacobum, and Iohannem, Iacobes broðor.

[And he suffered no man to follow him, save Peter, and James, and John the brother of James.]

38 And hi comon on ðæs heah-ealdres hus. And he geseah mycel gehyd, wepende and geomriende.
[And they came to the house of the ruler of the synagogue, and he saw the tumult, weeping and wailing.]

39 And ða he in-eode, he cwæþ, Hwi synd ge gedrefede, and wepaþ? Nis ðis mæden na dead, ac heo slæpþ.
[And when he went in, he said, Why make ye this ado, and weep? the damsel is not dead, but sleepeth.]

40 Ða tældon hi hine. He ða, eallum ut-adrifenum, nam ðæs mædenes fæder and moder, and ða ðe mid him wæron, and inn-eodon suwiende, ðar ðæt mæden wæs.
[Then they rebuked him. When he had put them all out, he took the father and the mother of the damsel, and those who were with him, and entereth in where the damsel was lying.]

41 And hire hand nam, and cwæþ, Thalimtha, cumi, ðæt is on ure geþeode gereht, Mæden, ðe ic secge, aris.
[And he took her hand, and said, Talitha cumi; which is interpreted for our people, Damsel, I say unto thee, arise.]

42 And heo sona aras, and eode; soþlice heo wæs twelf wintre. And ealle hi wundredon mycelre wundrunge.
[And straightway the damsel arose, and walked; for she was of the age of twelve years. And they all marvelled with a great astonishment.]

43 And he him þearle behead, ðæt hi hyt nanum men ne sædon. And he het hire etan syllan.
[And he charged them straitly that they should tell it to no man; and he commanded that something should be given her to eat.]

## 10.6 Quiz

### Translate from Anglo-Saxon into Modern English (1 point each)

1. ful — foul
2. heope — hip
3. crocca — pot
4. drenc — drink
5. ceafer — beetle
6. Scottas — Irishmen
7. tungol — constellation
8. biblioðece — bible
9. heahsæ — high seas
10. deadboren — stillborn
11. ðistel — thistle
12. snaw — snow
13. sunu — son
14. lytel — little
15. wæl — pool
16. widewe — widow
17. hore — whore
18. missan — to miss
19. smoð — smooth
20. grap — clutch
21. greatnes — greatness
22. clað — cloth
23. midrif — midriff
24. hwæt — listen! hey!
25. siex — six

### Translate from Modern English into Ango-Saxon (1 point each)

26. death — deað
27. whistling — hwistung
28. ancestor — ealdfæder
29. milk — meolc
30. distant — feorr
31. gold — gold
32. to wield — wieldan
33. spirit — gast
34. snake — snaca, wyrm
35. wood for a house — boldtimber
36. nightclothes — nihtwaru
37. brook — broc
38. claw — clea
39. smooth — smoð
40. fishhook — angil
41. sock — socc
42. mild — milde
43. mint — minte
44. nightlong — nihtlong
45. swan — swan
46. to smear — smerian
47. parable — bigspell
48. whelp — hwelp
49. church — cirice
50. spend the winter — oferwintrian

## Fill in the blanks (50 points, 5 points per blank)

51.

Hwæt! We **Gar-Đena** in geardagum,
**þeodcyninga**, þrym gefrunon,
hu ða æþelingas ellen **fremedon**.
Oft Scyld Scefing **sceaþena** þreatum,
**monegum** mægþum, meodosetla ofteah,
egsode eorlas. Syððan **ærest** wearð
**feasceaft** funden, he þæs frofre gebad,
weox under wolcnum, **weorðmyndum** þah,
oð þæt him æghwylc þara **ymbsittendra**
ofer hronrade hyran scolde,
gomban **gyldan**. þæt wæs god cyning!

[This page intentionally left blank]

# Chapter 11

# Translation (Part 3)

## Mark 6:14-29, Mark 6:30-45, Mark 8:1-13

### 11.2 Vocabulary Exercise

#### Translate the following phrases/sentences from modern English into Anglo-Saxon

1. up the iron post — up the iren post
2. holly on the tan comb — holen on the dunn camb
3. to kiss under the mistletoe — cyssan under the mistiltan
4. a thousand spears — a ðusund speres
5. to spew out the cold wine — spiwan ut the ceald win
6. Rome is sorry. — Romeburg is sarig.
7. to will none — willan nan
8. the potter's grey ring — the pottere's græg hring
9. a month of sour liver — a monað of sur lifer
10. merry monks on Monday — bliðe munucs on Monandæg
11. to prohibit a free fleet — forbeaodan a freo flota
12. aquatic monster of a distant land — brimwylf of a feorweg
13. tan stockings in the inn — dunn hosas in the gesthus
14. strength of the bumblebee — miht of the dora
15. Behold! the thumb of the giant! — Loc nu! the ðuma of the ent!
16. the thread of time — the ðræd of tima
17. the wild tiger's throat — the wilde tigris's ðrotu
18. precious freedom in the south — weorð freodom in the suð
19. the body's tears — the ban-hus's tears
20. the strong winch — the mihtig wince

## 11.3 Translation—Mark 6:14-29

14 And ða gehyrde Herodes se cyng, ðæt soþlice his nama wæs swutol geworden, and he cwæþ, Witodlice Iohannes se Fulluhtere of deaþe aras, and on him synd forðam mægenu geworht.

[And then king Herod heard that his name had become famous and he said, Surely John the Baptist has risen from the dead, and therefore mighty works are performed by him. ]

15 Sume cwædon, He is Elias; sume cwædon, He is witega, swylce an of ðam witegum.

[Some said, He is Elias. Some said, He is a wise man, or as one of the wise men. ]

16 Ða Herodes ðæt gehyrde, he cwæþ, Se Iohannes, ðe ic beheafdode, se aras of deaþe.

[When Herod heard it, he said, It is John, whom I beheaded: he is risen from the dead. ]

17 Soþlice Herodes sende, and het Iohannem, gebindan on cwerterne, for ðære Herodiadiscan, his broðor lafe, Philippus; forðam ðe he nam hi.

[For Herod himself sent forth and had John bound in prison for Herodias' sake, his brother Philip's widow: for he had married her. ]

18 Ða sæde Iohannes Herode, Nys ðe alyfed, to hæbbenne ðines broðer wif.

[Then John said unto Herod, It is not lawful for thee to have thy brother's wife. ]

19 Ða syrwde Herodias ymbe hine, and wolde hyne ofslean, and heo ne mihte.

[Then Herodias plotted against him, and wanted him killed; and she could not: ]

20 Soðlice Herodes ondred Iohannem, and wiste ðæt he wæs rihtwis and halig, and he heold hine on cwerterne. And he gehyrde ðæt he fela wundra worhte, and he lufelice him hyrde.

[For Herod feared John and knew that he was just and holy, and he held him in prison; and he heard that he did many wonders, and he heard him gladly. ]

21 Ða se dæg com Herodes gebyrdtide, he gegearwode mycele feorme his ealdormannum, and ðam fyrmestum on Galilea.

[And when the day of Herod's birthday was come, he made a great feast for his lords, and chief estates of Galilee; ]

22 And ða ða ðæra Herodiadiscan dohtor inn-eode. and tumbode, hit licode Herode, and eallum ðam ðe him mid sæton, se cing cwæþ ða to ðam mædene, Bide me swa hwæt swa ðu wylle, and ic ðe sylle.

[And when the daughter of Herodias came in. and danced, and it pleased Herod and them that sat with him, the king said unto the damsel, Ask of me whatsoever thou wilt, and I will give it thee. ]

23 And he swor hire, Soþes ic ðe sylle, swa hwæt swa ðu me bitst, ðeah ðu wylle healf min rice.

[And he sware unto her, Whatsoever thou shalt ask of me, truly I will give it thee, though you desire half of my kingdom. ]

24 Ða heo ut-eode, heo cwæþ to hyre meder, Hwæs bidde ic? Ða cwæþ heo, Iohannes heafod ðæs Fulluhteres.

[When she went forth, she said unto her mother, What shall I ask? Then she said, The head of John the Baptist. ]

25 Sona ða heo mid ofeste in to ðam cyninge eode, heo bæd, and ðus cwæþ, Ic wylle ðæt ðu me hrædlice on anum disce sylle Iohannes heafod.

[When she came in straightway with haste unto the king, she asked, and said thus, I will that thou give me quickly the head of John the Baptist on the platter. ]

26 Ða wearþ se cyning ge-unret forðam aþe, and forðam ðe him mid sæton nolde ðeah hi ge-unretan;

[Then the king grew sorry for his oath; yet for their sakes which sat with him, he would not disappoint her. ]

27 Ac sende ænne cwellere, and bebead ðæt man his heafod on anum disce brohte. And he hine ða on cwerterne beheafdode,

[But he sent an executioner, and commanded his head to be brought on a platter: and he went and beheaded him in the prison, ]

28 And his heafod on disce brohte, and hit sealde ðam mædene, and ðæt mæden hit sealde hire meder.

[And he brought his head on a platter, and gave it to the damsel: and the damsel gave it to her mother. ]

29 Ða his cnihtas ðæt gehyrdon, hi comon, and his lic namon, and hine on byrgene ledon.

[When his disciples heard it, they came and took up his corpse, and laid it in a tomb.]

## 11.4 Translation—Mark 6:30-45

30 Soþlice ða ða apostolas togædere comon, hi cyddon ðam Hælende eall, ðæt hi dydon, and hi lærdon.
[When the apostles gathered themselves together, they told the Savior all things, both what they had done, and what they had taught.]

31 And he sæde him, Cumaþ and uton gan on-sundron on weste stowe; and us hwon restan. Soþlice manega wæron ðe comon, and agen-hwyrfdon, and fyrst næfdon ðæt hi æton.
[And he said unto them, Come ye yourselves apart into a desert place, and let us rest a while: for there were many coming and going, and they had no leisure so much as to eat.]

32 And on scryp stigende, hi foron onsundron on weste stowe.
[And boarding a ship they departed into a desert place privately.]

33 And gesawon hi farende, and hi gecneowon manega, and gangende of ðam burgum, ðyder urnon, and him beforan comon.
[And they saw them departing, and many knew, and ran afoot thither out of their cities, and came together before him.]

34 And ða se Hælend ðanon eode he geseah mycele menegu, and he gemiltsode him, forðam ðe hi wæron swa swa scep ðe nanne hyrde nabbaþ. And he ongan hi fela læran.
[And when the Savior came out, saw much people, and was moved with compassion toward them, because they were as sheep who had no shepherd: and he began to teach them many things.]

35 And ða hit mycel ylding wæs, his leorning-cnihtas him to comon, and cwædon, Ðeos stow is weste, and tima is forþ-agan;
[And when the day was now far spent, his disciples came unto him, and said, This is a desert place, and now the time is far passed:]

36 Forlæt ðas manegu, ðæt hi faron on gehende tunas, and him mete bicgan ðæt hi eton.
[Send away the crowd, that they may go into the towns round about, and buy themselves food that they may eat.]

37 Ða cwæþ he, Sylle ge him etan. Ða cwædon hi, Uton gan and mid twam hundred penegum hlafas biegan, and we him etan syllaþ.
[Then he said, Give ye them to eat. Then they said, Shall we go and buy loaves with two hundred pennies, and give them to eat?]

38 Ða cwæþ he, Hu fela hlafa hæbba ge? Gaþ and lociaþ. And ða hi wiston, hi cwædon, Fif hlafas, and twegen fixas.
[Then said, How many loaves have ye? go and see. And when they knew, they said, Five loaves, and two fishes.]

39 And ða bebead se Hælend, ðæt ðæt fole sæte ofer ðæt grene hig.
[And then the Savior bad the people sit down upon the green grass.]

40 And hi ða sæton, hundredum, and fiftigum.
[And then they sat down, by hundreds, and by fifties.]

41 And fif hlafum, and twam fixum onfangenum, he on heofon locode, and hi bletsode, and ða hlafas bræc, and sealde his leorning-cnihtum, ðæt hi toforan him asetton. And twegen fixas him eallon dælde;
[And when he had taken the five loaves and the two fishes, he looked up to heaven, and blessed them, and brake the loaves, and gave them to his disciples to set them before them; and the two fishes divided he among them all.]

42 And hi æton ða ealle, and gefyllede wurdon.
[And they all ate, and were filled.]

43 And hi namon ðara hlafa, and fixa lafa, twelf wilian fulle.
[And they took up twelve baskets full of the loaves, and of the remaining fishes.]

44 Soþlice fif þusend manna, ðara etendra wæron.
[Indeed there were about five thousand men of those who ate.]

45 Ða sona he nydde his leorning-cnihtas on scyp stigan, ðæt hig him beforan foron ofer ðæne muþan to Bethsaida, oð he ðæt folc forlete.
[Straightway he constrained his disciples to get into the ship, that they should cross over the mouth unto Bethsaida, while he sent away the people.]

## 11.5 Translation—Mark 8:1-13

1 Eft on ðam dagum, him wæs mid micel menigu, and næfdon hwæt hi æton, ða cwæþ he, to somne geclypedum his leorning-cnihtum,
[Again, in those days a great multitude was with him, and they had nothing to eat. Then Jesus called his disciples unto him, and said unto them,]

2 Ic gemiltsige ðysse menegu, forðam hi þry dagas me ge-anbidiaþ, and nabbaþ hwæt hi eton;
[I have compassion on this multitude, because they have now been with me three days, and have nothing to eat:]

3 Gif ic hi fæstende to hyra husum læte, be wege hi geteorigeaþ; sume hi comon feorran.
[If I send them away fasting to their own houses, they will faint by the way: for some of them came from far.]

4 And ða andswarodon him his leorning-cnihtas, Hwanon mæg ænig man ðas mid hlafum on ðisum westene gefyllan?
[And then his disciples answered him, From whence can any man satisfy these men with bread here in the wilderness?]

5 Ða axode he hi, Hu fela hlafa hæbbe ge? Hi cwædon, Seofon.
[And he asked them, How many loaves have ye? And they said, Seven.]

6 Ða het he sittan ða menegu ofer ða eorþan. And nam ða seofon hlafas, and Gode þancode, and hi bræc, and sealde his leorning-cnihtum, ðæt hi toforan him asetton. And hi swa dydon.
[And he commanded the people to sit down on the ground: and he took the seven loaves, and thanked God, and brake them, and gave to his disciples to set them before them; and they did so.]

7 And hi næfdon buton feawa fixa; and he ða bletsode, and het beforan him settan.
[And they had a few fishes: and he them blessed, and commanded to set them also before them.]

8 And hi æton, and wurdon gefyllede; and hi namon ðæt of ðam brytsenum belaf, seofon wilian fulle.
[So they did eat, and were filled: and they took up of the broken meat that was left seven baskets.]

9 Soþlice ða ðe ðar æton, wæron fif þusend; and he hi ða forlet.
[And they that ate were four thousand: and he sent them away.]

10 And sona he on scyp, mid his leorning-cnihtum, astah, and com on ða dælas Dalmanuþa.
[And straightway he entered into a ship with his disciples, and came into the parts of Dalmanutha.]

11 And ða ferdon ða Pharisei, and ongunnon mid him smeagean, and tacen of heofone sohton, and his fandedon.
[And then the Pharisees came forth, and began to question with him, and sought a sign from heaven, and tested him.]

12 Ða cwæþ he, geomriende on his gaste, Hwi secþ ðeos cneoris tacen? Soþlice ic eow secge, ne biþ ðisse cneorisse tacen geseald.
[Then sighing in his spirit, he said, Why doth this generation seek after a sign? verily I say unto you, There shall no sign be given unto this generation.]

13 And hi ða forlætende, eft on scyp astah, and ferde ofer ðone muþan.
[And then leaving them, he entered again into the ship and departed over the mouth.]

## 11.6 Quiz

### Translate from Anglo-Saxon into Modern English (1 point each)

1. monað — month
2. hnitu — louse egg
3. hring — ring
4. flota — fleet
5. spiwan — vomit
6. ðrotu — throat
7. ðuma — thumb
8. freo — free
9. willan — to will
10. drypan — to drip
11. halig — holy
12. ðusund — thousand
13. Romeburg — Rome
14. forbeodan — prohibit
15. tigris — tiger
16. cyssan — kiss
17. folclagu — common law
18. græg — grey
19. haligwæter — holy water
20. ent — giant
21. grap — clutch
22. angil — fish-hook
23. ðritig — thirty
24. heahsæ — high seas
25. plyme — plum

### Translate from Modern English into Ango-Saxon (1 point each)

26. windy — windig
27. broth — broð
28. aquatic monster — brimwylf
29. soul — sawol
30. merry — bliðe
31. spark — speare
32. cold — ceald
33. precious — weorð
34. mistletoe — mistiltan
35. stocking — hosa
36. England — Englalond
37. behold! — loc nu!
38. common law — folclagu
39. bumblebee — dora
40. inn — gesthus
41. distant land — feorr land
42. winch — wince
43. wild — wilde
44. fisherman — fiscere
45. throat — ðrotu
46. to sit — sittan
47. midsummer — middansumer
48. lisp — wlips
49. empty — æmtig
50. horn — horn

## Fill in the blanks (50 points, 2.5 points per blank)

51.

Hwæt! **We** Gar-Ðena in **geardagum**,
þeodcyninga, **þrym** gefrunon,
**hu** ða æþelingas **ellen** fremedon.
**Oft** Scyld Scefing **sceaþena** þreatum,
monegum **mægþum**, meodosetla **ofteah**,
**egsode** eorlas. Syððan **ærest** wearð
feasceaft **funden**, he þæs frofre **gebad**,
**weox** under **wolcnum**, weorðmyndum **þah**,
oð þæt him æghwylc **þara** ymbsittendra
ofer hronrade **hyran** scolde,
gomban **gyldan**. þæt wæs god **cyning**!

[This page intentionally left blank]

# Chapter 12

# Translation (Part Four)

### Mark 8:14-26, Mark 8:27-38, Mark 10:1-12

## 12.2 Vocabulary Exercises

### Translate the following phrases/sentences from Modern English into Anglo-Saxon

1. to freeze the stream — freosan the stream
2. to come to the ford today — (be)cuman to the ford todæg
3. home on Friday morning — ham on Frigedæg morgen
4. the magic word of the moor in the wasteland — the galdorword of the mor in the westen
5. to spill honey on the wise lobster — (ge)spillan hunig on the wis lopystre
6. a foolish swarm of bees — a stunt beogang
7. the truth about toads — the treow about tades
8. to tire at once — teorian instæpe
9. to spit at the moon — spittian at the mona
10. to wink at the priest — wincian at the preost
11. rosy morning light — rosen morgenleoht
12. a grim drop from the stairs of the stronghold

    — a grimm dropa from the stæger of the burg / ceaster / fæsten
13. the hoof over the oven — the hof ofer the ofen
14. to spin a long line — (ge)spinnan a lang line
15. the mood of the midge tomorrow — the mod of the gnæt tomergen
16. the correct herb — the rigt wyrt
17. the eternal cold of the north — the sincaldu of the norð
18. a pound of tinder — the pund of tynder
19. to stand below the stars — (ge)standan below the steorras
20. a capital offense against the provincial governor — a deaðscyld against the ealdorman

## 12.3 Translation—Mark 8:14-26

14 And hi ofergeton ðæt hi hlafas ne namon, and hi næfdon on scype mid him buton ænne hlaf.

[And they forgot to take bread, neither had they in the ship with them more than one loaf.]

15 And he him bead, and cwæþ, Lociaþ, and warniaþ fram Pharisea, and Herodes hæfe.

[And he charged them, and said, Take heed, beware of the leaven of the Pharisees, and of the leaven of Herod. ]

16 Ða þohton, hi betwux him, and cwædon, Næbbe we nane hlafas.

[Then they reasoned among themselves, and said, We have no bread.]

17 Ða se Hælend ðæt wiste, he cwæþ, Hwæt þence ge, forðam ge hlafas nabbaþ? Gyt ge ne oncnawaþ, ne ne ongytaþ; gyt ge habbaþ eowre heortan geblende.

[When the Savior knew it, he said, Why reason ye, because ye have no bread? perceive ye not yet, neither understand? have ye your heart yet hardened?]

18 Eagan ge habbaþ, and ne geseoþ, and earan, and ne gehyraþ; ne ge ne þencaþ,

[Do you have eyes, and see ye not? and ears, and hear ye not? and do ye not remember?]

19 Hwænne ic bræc fif hlafas and twegen fixas, and hu fela wyligena ge namon fulle? Hi cwædon ða, Twelfe.

[When I brake the five loaves and two fishes, how many baskets full of fragments took ye up? Then they said, Twelve.]

20 And hwænne seofon hlafas feower þusendum, and hu fela wyligena brytsena ge namon fulle? Hi sædon, Seofon.

[And when the seven among four thousand, how many baskets full of fragments took ye up? They said, Seven.]

21 Ða sæde he him, Hwi ne ongyte ge gyt?

[Then he said unto them, How is it that ye do not understand?]

22 And hi comon ða to Bethzaida, and hi brohton him ða ænne blindne, and hine bædon, ðæt he hine æt-hrine.

[And they came to Bethsaida; and then they brought a blind man unto him, and besought him to touch him.]

23 And ða æt-hran he ðæs blindan hand, and lædde hine butan ða wic, and spætte on his eagan, and his hand onasette, and hine axode, hwæðer he aht gesawe.

[And then he took the blind man's hand, and led him out of the town; and spat on his eyes, and put his hand upon him, and asked him if he saw ought.]

24 Ða cwæð he ða, ða he hyne beseah, Ic geseo men swylce treow gangende.

[Then he said, when he looked up, I see men as trees, walking.]

25 Eft he asette his handa ofer his eagan, and he geseah ða, and wearþ geedniwod, swa ðæt he beorhtlice eall geseah.

[Again he put his hands again upon his eyes, and made him look up: and he was restored, and saw every thing clearly.]

26 Ða sende he hyne to his huse, and cwæþ, Ga to ðinum huse; and ðeah ðu on tun ga, nænegum ðu hit ne sege.

[Then he sent him away to his house, and said, Go to your house; and though you go into the town, do not tell it to anyone. ]

## 12.4 Translation—Mark 8:27-38

27 Ða eode he and his leorning-cnihtas on ðæt castel Cesareæ Philippi. And he on wege his leorning-cnihtas ahsode, Hwæt secgaþ men ðæt ic sy?
[Then he and his disciples went into the town of Caesarea Philippi: and by the way he asked his disciples, What do men say that I am? ]

28 Ða andswarodon hi, Sume, Iohannem ðone Fulluhtere; sume, Heliam; sume, sumne of ðam witegum.
[Then they answered, Some, John the Baptist: but some, Elias; and some, One of the prophets.]

29 Ða cwæþ he, Hwæt secge ge ðæt ic sy? Ða andswarode Petrus him, and cwæþ, Ðu eart Crist.
[Then he saith unto them, What say ye that I am? And Peter answereth and saith, Thou art the Christ.]

30 And ða bead he him, ðæt hi nænegum be him ne sædon.
[And then he bad them that they should tell no man of him.]

31 Ða ongan he hi læran, ðat mannes sunu gebyreþ fela þinga þolian, and beon aworpen fram ealdormannum, and heahsacerdum, and bocerum, and beon ofslegen, and æfter þrim dagum arisan.
[Then he began to teach them, that the Son of man must suffer many things, and be rejected of the elders, and of the chief priests, and scribes, and be killed, and after three days rise.]

32 And spræc ða openlice. And ða nam Petrus hine, and ongan hine þreagean.
[And he spake that saying openly. And then Peter took him, and began to rebuke him.]

33 Ða bewende he hine, and cidde Petre, and cwæþ, Ga onbæc, Satanas; forðam ðu nast ða þing ðe synd Godes, ac ða þing ðe synd manna.
[Then he turned about and rebuked Peter, and said, Go back, Satan: for thou do not know the things that be of God, but the things that be of men.]

34 Ða cwæþ he, togædere geclypedre menegu, mid his leorning-cnihtum, Gif hwa wyle me fyligean, wiðsace hine sylfne, and nime his cwylminge, and folgige me.
[When he had called the people unto him with his disciples also, he said, If anyone wished to follow me, let him deny himself, and take up his cross, and follow me. ]

35 Se ðe wyle his sawle hale gedon, se hi forspilþ; se ðe forspilþ his sawle for me and for ðam godspelle se hig gehælþ.
[He who wishes to save his soul shall lose it; he who shall lose his soul for me and for the gospel, the same shall save it.]

36 Hwæt fremaþ men, ðeah he eallne middan-eard gestryne, and do his sawle forwyrd?
[For what shall it profit a man, if he shall gain the whole world, and bring about death for his soul?]

37 Oððe hwylc gewryxl sylþ se man for his sawle?
[Or what shall a man give in exchange for his soul? ]

38 Soþlice se ðe me forsyhþ, and mine word on ðisre unriht-hæmedan and synfulran cneorisse, ðone mannes sunu forsyhþ, ðonne he cymþ on his fæder wuldre, mid halgum englum
[Whosoever therefore shall scorn me and my word in this adulterous and sinful generation; him shall the Son of Man scorn, when he cometh in the glory of his Father with the holy angels]

## 12.5 Translation—Mark 10:1-12

1 And ðanon, he com on Iudeisce endas of Iordane; ða comon eft menigu to him, and swa swa he gewunode, he hi lærde eft-sona.

[And he arose from thence, and cometh into the coasts of Judaea by the farther side of Jordan: and the people resort unto him again; and, as he was wont, he taught them again.[

2 Ða genealæhton him Pharisei, and hine axodon, Hwæðer alyfþ ænegum men his wif forlætan? his ðus fandigende.

[And the Pharisees came to him, and asked him, Is it lawful for a man to put away his wife? tempting him.]

3 Ða andswarode he him, Hwæt bead Moyses eow?

[And he answered and said unto them, What did Moses command you?]

4 Hi sædon, Moyses lyfde ðæt man write hiw-gedales boc, and hi forlete.

[And they said, Moses suffered to write a bill of divorcement, and to put her away]

5 Ða cwæþ se Hælend, For eowre heortan heardnesse he eow wrat ðis bebod.

[And Jesus answered and said unto them, For the hardness of your heart he wrote you this precept.]

6 Fram fruman gesceafte God hi geworhte wæpnedman and wimman;

[But from the beginning of the creation God made them male and female.]

7 And cwæþ, Forðam se man forlæt his fæder and moder, and hine his wife geðeot,

[And he said, for this cause shall a man leave his father and mother, and cleave to his wife;]

8 And beoþ twegen on anum flæsce. Witodlice ne synd na twegen, ac an flæsc.

[And they twain shall be one flesh: truly they are no more twain, but one flesh.]

9 Ðæt God gesamnode, ne syndrige ðæt nan man.

[What therefore God hath joined together, let not man put asunder.]

10 And eft innan huse his leorning-cnihtas hine be ðam ylcan ahsodon.

[And in the house his disciples asked him of the same matter.]

11 Ða cwæþ he, Swa hwylc man swa his wif forlæt, and oðer nimþ, unrihthæmed he wyrcþ þurh hi.

[Then he said, Whosoever shall put away his wife, and marry another, committeth adultery against her.]

12 And gif ðæt wif hire were forlæt, and oðerne nimþ, heo unriht-hæmþ.

[And if a woman shall put away her husband, and be married to another, she committeth adultery.]

[This page intentionally left blank]

## 12.6 QUIZ

### Translate from Anglo-Saxon into Modern English (1 point each)

1. ford — ford
2. tomergen — tomorrow
3. beam — log
4. ealdorman — provincial governor
5. tade — toad
6. preost — priest
7. hrof — roof
8. (ge)standan — to stand
9. (be)cuman — to come
10. wyrt — herb
11. wincian — to wink
12. Frigedæg — Friday
13. ta — toe
14. spittian — to spit
15. norð — north
16. freosan — to freeze
17. stæger — stairs
18. morgenleoht — morning light
19. lopystre — lobster
20. lang — long
21. feorweg — distant land
22. miht — strength
23. bliðe — merry
24. sarig — sorry
25. win — wine

### Translate from Modern English into Ango-Saxon (1 point each)

26. island — igland
27. honey — hunig
28. to tire — teorian
29. drop — dropa
30. moon — mona
31. winsome — wynsum
32. home — ham
33. at once — instæpe
34. wise — wis
35. knee — cneow
36. morning — morgen
37. eternal cold — sincaldu
38. stronghold — burg, ceaster, fæsten
39. tongs — (ge)tang
40. stammer — stamerian
41. rosy — rosen
42. capital offense — deaðscyld
43. today — todæg
44. swarm of bees — beogang
45. foolish — stunt
46. iron — iren
47. sour — sur
48. potter — pottere
49. hilt — hilt
50. holly — holen

## Fill in the blanks (50 points, 5 points per blank)

51.

Hwæt! We Gar-Đena in **geardagum,**
þeodcyninga, **þrym** gefrunon,
hu ða æþelingas **ellen** fremedon.
Oft **Scyld** Scefing sceaþena þreatum,
monegum mægþum, **meodosetla** ofteah,
**egsode** eorlas. Syððan ærest wearð
feasceaft funden, he þæs frofre **gebad,**
**weox** under wolcnum, weorðmyndum þah,
**oð þæt** him æghwylc þara ymbsittendra
ofer **hronrade** hyran scolde,
gomban gyldan. þæt wæs god cyning!

[This page intentionally left blank]

[This page intentionally left blank]

# Chapter 13

# Beowulf

## Beowulf 1-11, Beowulf 12-25, Beowulf 99-114

### 13.2 Vocabulary Exercise

#### Translate the following phrases/sentences from Modern English into Anglo-Saxon

1. horse's tongue — hors's tunge
2. land of the English — land / eard of the Englisc
3. to hop on the worm in the dust — hoppan on the wyrm in the dust
4. friendless horse-handler on the knoll — freondleas horsðegn
5. most moths in Norway — mæst moððes in Norðweg
6. to stare at the stepmother's nose — starian at the steopmodor's nosu
7. to row with the carpenter's tool — rowan wiþ the treowyrhta's tol
8. to sting like a hornet — stingan like a hyrnetu
9. the trap in the still tower — the træppe in the stille torr
10. to tread like a wolf — tredan like a wulf
11. wit of the big, beloved stepson — witt of the great/micel, leof steopsunu
12. the correct law of the district — the riht lagu of the scir
13. a country's just protector — a land's riht helm
14. monastery in the fog — mynster in the mist
15. to steer the course of events — styran the wyrd
16. to grind with steel — grindan wiþ style
17. comely stepdaughter is a wonder — cymlic steopdohtor is a wunder
18. friend of the spider — freond of the attorcoppe
19. the starling on a hook — the stær(ling) on a hoc
20. the stiff provost with his friend and his flute

    — the stif profost wiþ his freond and his hwistle

## 13.3 Translation—Beowulf 1-11 (Prologue Part 1)

### Anglo-Saxon

Hwæt! We Gar-Ðena  in geardagum,
þeodcyninga,  þrym gefrunon,
hu ða æþelingas  ellen fremedon.
Oft Scyld Scefing  sceaþena þreatum,
monegum mægþum,  meodosetla ofteah,
egsode eorle.  Syððan ærest wearð
feasceaft funden,  he þæs frofre gebad,
weox under wolcnum,  weorðmyndum þah,
oð þæt him æghwylc  þara ymbsittendra
ofer hronrade  hyran scolde,
gomban gyldan.  þæt wæs god cyning!

### English

Lo! the Spear-Danes' glory through splendid achievements
The folk-kings' former fame we have heard of,
How princes displayed then their prowess-in-battle.
Oft Scyld the Scefing from scathers in numbers
From many a people their mead-benches tore.
Since first he found him friendless and wretched,
The earl had had terror: comfort he got for it,
Waxed 'neath the welkin, world-honor gained,
Till all his neighbors o'er sea were compelled to
Bow to his bidding and bring him their tribute:
An excellent atheling!

## 13.4 Translation—Beowulf 12-25 (Prologue Part 2)

### Anglo-Saxon

ðæm eafera wæs    æfter cenned,
geong in geardum,    þone god sende
folce to frofre;    fyrenðearfe ongeat
þe hie ær drugon    aldorlease
lange hwile.    Him þæs liffrea,
wuldres wealdend,    woroldare forgeaf;
Beow wæs breme    (blæd wide sprang),
Scyldes eafera    Scedelandum in.
Swa sceal geong guma    gode gewyrcean,
fromum feohgiftum    on fæder bearme,
þæt hine on ylde    eft gewunigen
wilgesiþas,    þonne wig cume,
leode gelæsten;    lofdædum sceal
in mægþa gehwære    man geþeon.

### English

After was borne him
A son and heir, young in his dwelling,
Whom God-Father sent to solace the people.
He had marked the misery malice had caused them,
That reaved of their rulers they wretched had erstwhile
Long been afflicted. The Lord, in requital,
Wielder of Glory, with world-honor blessed him.
Famed was Beowulf, far spread the glory
Of Scyld's great son in the lands of the Danemen.
So the carle that is young, by kindnesses rendered
The friends of his father, with fees in abundance
Must be able to earn that when age approacheth
Eager companions aid him requitingly,
When war assaults him serve him as liegemen:
By praise-worthy actions must honor be got
'Mong all of the races.

## 13.5 Translation—Beowulf 99-114 (Grendel, Descendant of Cain)

### Anglo-Saxon

Swa ða drihtguman dreamum lifdon
eadiglice, oð ðæt an ongan
fyrene fremman feond on helle.
Wæs se grimma gæst Grendel haten,
mære mearcstapa, se þe moras heold,
fen ond fæsten; fifelcynnes eard
wonsæli wer weardode hwile,
siþðan him scyppend forscrifen hæfde
in Caines cynne. Þone cwealm gewræc
ece drihten, þæs þe he Abel slog;
ne gefeah he þære fæhðe, ac he hine feor forwræc,
metod for þy mane, mancynne fram.
Þanon untydras ealle onwocon,
eotenas ond ylfe ond orcneas,
swylce gigantas, þa wið gode wunnon
lange þrage; he him ðæs lean forgeald.

### English

So blessed with abundance, brimming with joyance,
The warriors abided, till a certain one gan to
Dog them with deeds of direfullest malice,
A foe in the hall-building: this horrible stranger [1]
Was Grendel entitled, the march-stepper famous
Who dwelt in the moor-fens, the marsh and the fastness;
The wan-mooded being abode for a season
In the land of the giants, when the Lord and Creator
Had banned him and branded. For that bitter murder,
The killing of Abel, all-ruling Father
Cain is referred to as a progenitor of Grendel, and of monsters in general.
The kindred of Cain crushed with His vengeance;
In the feud He rejoiced not, but far away drove him
From kindred and kind, that crime to atone for,
Meter of Justice. Thence ill-favored creatures,
Elves and giants, monsters of ocean,
Came into being, and the giants that longtime
Grappled with God; He gave them requital.



1. As Lesslie Hall points out in his translation, some authorities would translate this 'demon' instead of 'stranger.'

## 13.6 Quiz

### Translate from Anglo-Saxon into Modern English (1 point each)

1. eard — land
2. wundor — wondor
3. starian — to stare
4. wordriht — correct word
5. wyrm — worm
6. helm — protector
7. steopdohtor — stepdaughter
8. hyrnetu — hronet
9. ule — owl
10. ripe — ripe
11. stær(ling) — starling
12. cnoll — knoll
13. rowan — to row
14. Norðweg — Norway
15. modor — mother
16. unfæst — loose
17. torr — tower
18. Englisc — English
19. mynster — monastery
20. wyrd — course of events
21. beogang — swarm of bees
22. wincian — to wink
23. steorra — star
24. sprott — sprout
25. tynder — tinder

### Translate from Modern English into Ango-Saxon (1 point each)

26. wit — witt
27. to hop — hoppan
28. comely — cymlic
29. horse-handler — horsðegn
30. woman — wif
31. friendless — freondleas
32. atom — mot
33. provost — profost
34. correct law — riht lagu
35. district — scir
36. tongue — tunge
37. beloved — leof
38. stepfather — steopfæder
39. carpenter — treowyrhta
40. flute — hwistle
41. spider — attorcoppe
42. fog — mist
43. wool — wull
44. country — land
45. to tread — tredan
46. spur — spura
47. stream — stream
48. hood — nod
49. grim — grimm
50. Friday — Frigedæg

## Fill in the blanks (50 points, 2.5 points per blank)

51.

**Hwæt!** We **Gar-Đena** in geardagum,
**Þeodcyninga**, þrym **gefrunon**,
hu ða **æþelingas** ellen **fremedon**.
Oft Scyld **Scefing** sceaþena **Þreatum**,
**monegum** mægþum, **meodosetla** ofteah,
egsode eorlas. **Syððan** ærest wearð
**feasceaft** funden, he þæs **frofre** gebad,
weox under **wolcnum**, **weorðmyndum** þah,
oð þæt him **æghwylc** þara **ymbsittendra**
ofer **hronrade** hyran scolde,
gomban gyldan. þæt wæs **god** cyning!

# Chapter 14

# Translation Part 2

## Beowulf 710-19, Beowulf 720-30, Beowulf 815-23, 833-36

## 14.2 Vocabulary Exercises

### Translate the following phrases/sentences from Modern English into Anglo-Saxon

1. while butter from the cow — þenden butere fram / of the cu
2. a crab on the cot — a crabba on the cradol
3. louse eggs from the frost — hnitu fram / of the forst
4. to mow over the mound — mawan over the cnoll
5. to stoop beneath the ground — stupian beneath the grund
6. a stool near the bookcase — a stol near the bocfodder
7. the worth of a brother's crown — the weorð of a broðor's corona / cynehelm
8. the strawberry on the hot stove in the fort

   — the streaberge on the hat stofa / ofn in the burg / ceaster
9. A blow to the ear is a wound. — an earslege is a wund
10. drowsiness of an evening in autumn — hnappung of an æfentid in hærfest
11. psalm in the English language and runes — sealm in Englisc and run
12. drunken frog in the current — druncen frogga in the (brim) stream
13. to fracture a bone with a stone — brecan a ban wiþ a stan
14. how to grin not at all like a mouse — hu grennian no like a mus
15. fragrance of dung in the nostrils — stenc of tord in the nosþyrls
16. Nota bene! The logic and cunning of the louse!

    — Loc nu! The flitcræft and orðonc of the lus!
17. to mourn with a loud mouth — murnan wiþ a hlud muð
18. the grip of a hundred knots — the grap of a hund cnottas
19. the curve-prowed ship from the evil mountain — the hringedstefna fram / of the yfel munt
20. meanwhile to become pimply — þenden pypelian

## 14.3 Translation—Beowulf 710-19 (Grendel Attacks the Hall)

### Anglo-Saxon

ða com of more   under misthleoþum
Grendel gongan,   godes yrre bær;
mynte se manscaða   manna cynnes
sumne besyrwan   in sele þam hean.
Wod under wolcnum   to þæs þe he winreced,
goldsele gumena,   gearwost wisse,
fættum fahne.   Ne wæs þæt forma sið
þæt he Hroþgares   ham gesohte;
næfre he on aldordagum   ær ne siþðan
heardran hæle,   healðegnas fand.

### English

'Neath the cloudy cliffs came from the moor then
Grendel going, God's anger bare he.
The monster intended some one of earthmen
In the hall-building grand to entrap and make way with:
He went under welkin where well he knew of
The wine-joyous building, brilliant with plating,
Gold-hall of earthmen. Not the earliest occasion
He the home and manor of Hrothgar had sought:
Ne'er found he in life-days later nor earlier
Hardier hero, hall-thanes more sturdy!

## 14.4 Translation—Beowulf 720-30 (Grendel Attacks the Hall)

### Anglo-Saxon

Com þa to recede    rinc siðian,
dreamum bedæled.    Duru sona onarn,
fyrbendum fæst,    syþðan he hire folmum æthran;
onbræd þa bealohydig,    ða he gebolgen wæs,
recedes muþan.    Raþe æfter þon
on fagne flor    feond treddode,
eode yrremod;    him of eagum stod
ligge gelicost    leoht unfæger.
Geseah he in recede    rinca manige,
swefan sibbegedriht    samod ætgædere,
magorinca heap.

### English

Then came to the building the warrior marching,
His horrid fingers tear the door open.
Bereft of his joyance. The door quickly opened
On fire-hinges fastened, when his fingers had touched it;
The fell one had flung then—his fury so bitter—
Open the entrance. Early thereafter
The foeman trod the shining hall-pavement,
Strode he angrily; from the eyes of him glimmered
A lustre unlovely likest to fire.
He beheld in the hall the heroes in numbers,
A circle of kinsmen sleeping together,
A throng of thanemen.

## 14.5 Translation—Beowulf 815-23, 833-36 (Grendel's Defeat)

### Anglo-Saxon

Licsar gebad
atol æglæca; him on eaxle wearð
syndolh sweotol, seonowe onsprungon,
burston banlocan. Beowulfe wearð
guðhreð gyfeþe; scolde Grendel þonan
feorhseoc fleon under fenhleoðu,
secean wynleas wic; wiste þe geornor
þæt his aldres wæs ende gegongen,
dogera dægrim.
…
þæt wæs tacen sweotol,
syþðan hildedeor hond alegde,
earm ond eaxle (þær wæs eal geador
Grendles grape) under geapne hrof.

### English

A body-wound suffered
The direful demon, damage incurable
Was seen on his shoulder, his sinews were shivered,
His body did burst. To Beowulf was given
Glory in battle; Grendel from thenceward
Must flee and hide him in the fen-cliffs and marshes,
Sick unto death, his dwelling must look for
Unwinsome and woful; he wist the more fully
The end of his earthly existence was nearing,
His life-days' limits.
…
'Twas a manifest token,
When the hero-in-battle the hand suspended,
The arm and the shoulder (there was all of the claw
Of Grendel together) 'neath great-stretching hall-roof.

## 14.6 Quiz

### Translate from Anglo-Saxon to Modern English (1 point each)

1. streaberge — strawberry
2. tord — dung
3. munt — mountain
4. stupian — to stoop
5. muð — mouth
6. cynehelm — crown
7. cnotta — knot
8. hu — how
9. yfel — evil
10. cradol — cot
11. bocfodder — bookcase
12. treow — tree
13. hnappung — drowsiness
14. druncen — drunk
15. ceaster — fort
16. timber — timber
17. weorð — worth
18. stenc — fragrance
19. pypelian — to become pimply
20. orðonc — cunning
21. land — land, country
22. wullen — made of wool
23. bor — drill
24. style — steel
25. hyrnetu — hornet

### Translate from Modern English to Anglo-Saxon (1 point each)

26. rune — run
27. frost — forst
28. cow — cu
29. to mow — mawan
30. house — hus
31. English language — Englisc
32. blow to the ear — earslege
33. nostril — nosþyrl
34. evening — æfentid
35. current — (brim)stream
36. crossmember — eaxlgespan
37. brother — broðor
38. louse eggs — hnitu
39. autumn — hærfest
40. to fracture a bone — brecan
41. stone — stan
42. curve-prowed ship — hringedstefna
43. fort — burg / ceaster
44. trough — trog
45. logic — flitcræft
46. ripe — ripe
47. foolish — stunt
48. winsome — wynsum
49. stairs — stæger
50. hoof — hof

## Fill in the blanks (50 points, 2 points per blank)

51.

**Hwæt**! We **Gar-Đena** in geardagum,
**Þeodcyninga**, þrym **gefrunon**,
**hu** ða **æpelingas** ellen **fremedon**.
**Oft** Scyld Scefing sceaþena **Þreatum**,
**monegum** mægþum, **meodosetla** ofteah,
**egsode** eorlas. **Syððan** ærest wearð
**feasceaft** funden, **he** þæs frofre gebad,
**weox** under wolcnum, **weorðmyndum** þah,
**oð þæt** him æghwylc þara **ymbsittendra**
**ofer** hronrade **hyran** scolde,
**gomban** gyldan. **þæt** wæs **god** cyning!

# Chapter 15

# Translation (Part 3)

## Beowulf 1537-56, Beowulf 2309-23, Beowulf 2694-2715

## 15.2 Vocabulary Exercises

### Translate the following phrases/sentences from Modern English into Anglo-Saxon

1. to suck the rind of the cucumber – sucan the rind of the eorðæppel
2. twin butterfly on the rose – getwinn buterfleoge on the rose
3. to swim further than a furlong – swimman fuðor than a furhlang
4. to sweat for bread with hunger in the gut – swætan for hlaf wiþ hungor in the guttas
5. the dwelling of the insect – the inn of the wyrm
6. sweat under the sun – swat under the sunne
7. to swing with the twelfth sword – swingan wiþ the twelfta sweord
8. to cut one's hair for fuel – efsian for tynder
9. pure purple dye for the cradle – clæne purpure for the cradol
10. twelve hunters in the eye of the storm – twelf huntas in the eage of the storm
11. to twinkle as a sunbeam – twinclian swa a sunbeam
12. to sweep with two rough brambles – swapan wiþ tu / twa unsmeðe brembers
13. the sweet honeycomb in the psalter – the swete beebread in the saltere
14. to write a story of murder – writan a spell of morðor
15. to subdue the hungry mule – ofercuman the hungrig mul
16. mucus from twenty swine – snofl / snot fram / of twentig swin
17. "Nut" is a noun. – "Hnut" is a nama
18. a string of puzzles – a streng of cnottas
19. psalm-singing in the summer – sealmsong in the sumor
20. to hunt with guilt for oysters in the swamp – huntian wiþ gylt for ostres in the fenn

## 15.3 Translation—Beowulf 1537-56 (Fight with Grendel's Mother)

### Anglo-Saxon

Gefeng þa be eaxle    (nalas for fæhðe mearn)
Guðgeata leod    Grendles modor;
brægd þa beadwe heard,    þa he gebolgen wæs,
feorhgeniðlan,    þæt heo on flet gebeah.
Heo him eft hraþe    andlean forgeald
grimman grapum    ond him togeanes feng;
oferwearp þa werigmod    wigena strengest,
feþecempa,    þæt he on fylle wearð.
Ofsæt þa þone selegyst    ond hyre seax geteah,
brad ond brunecg,    wolde hire bearn wrecan,
angan eaferan.    Him on eaxle læg
breostnet broden;    þæt gebearh feore,
wið ord ond wið ecge    ingang forstod.
Hæfde ða forsiðod    sunu Ecgþeowes
under gynne grund,    Geata cempa,
nemne him heaðobyrne    helpe gefremede,
herenet hearde,    ond halig god
geweold wigsigor;    witig drihten,
rodera rædend,    hit on ryht gesced
yðelice,    syþðan he eft astod.

## English

The lord of the War-Geats
(He shrank not from battle) seized by the shoulder
The mother of Grendel; then mighty in struggle
Swung he his enemy, since his anger was kindled,
That she fell to the floor. With furious grapple
Beowulf falls.
She gave him requital early thereafter,
And stretched out to grab him; the strongest of warriors
Faint-mooded stumbled, till he fell in his traces,
The monster sits on him with drawn sword.
Foot-going champion. Then she sat on the hall-guest
And wielded her war-knife wide-bladed, flashing,
For her son would take vengeance, her one only bairn.
His armor saves his life.
His breast-armor woven bode on his shoulder;
It guarded his life, the entrance defended
'Gainst sword-point and edges. Ecgtheow's son there
Had fatally journeyed, champion of Geatmen,
In the arms of the ocean, had the armor not given,
Close-woven corslet, comfort and succor,
God arranged for his escape.
And had God most holy not awarded the victory,
All-knowing Lord; easily did heaven's
Ruler most righteous arrange it with justice;
Uprose he erect ready for battle.

## 15.4 Translation—Beowulf 2309-23 (The Dragon Ravages the Land)

### Anglo-Saxon

Wæs se fruma egeslic
leodum on lande, swa hyt lungre wearð
on hyra sincgifan sare geendod.
ða se gæst ongan gledum spiwan,
beorht hofu bærnan; bryneleoma stod
eldum on andan. No ðær aht cwices
lað lyftfloga læfan wolde.
Wæs þæs wyrmes wig wide gesyne,
nearofages nið nean ond feorran,
hu se guðsceaða Geata leode
hatode ond hynde. hord eft gesceat,
dryhtsele dyrnne, ær dæges hwile.
Hæfde landwara lige befangen,
bæle ond bronde, beorges getruwode,
wiges ond wealles; him seo wen geleah.

## English

Fearful the start was
To earls in the land, as it early thereafter
To their giver-of-gold was grievously ended.
The stranger began then to vomit forth fire,
To burn the great manor; the blaze then glimmered
For anguish to earlmen, not anything living
Was the hateful air-goer willing to leave there.
The war of the worm widely was noticed,
The feud of the foeman afar and anear,
How the enemy injured the earls of the Geatmen,
Harried with hatred: back he hied to the treasure,
To the well-hidden cavern ere the coming of daylight.
He had circled with fire the folk of those regions,
With brand and burning; in the barrow he trusted,
In the wall and his war-might: the weening deceived him.

## 15.5 Translation—Beowulf 2694-2715

### (Beowulf and Wiglaf Defeat the Dragon)

### Anglo-Saxon

ða ic æt þearfe gefrægn    þeodcyninges
andlongne eorl    ellen cyðan,
cræft ond cenðu,    swa him gecynde wæs.
Ne hedde he þæs heafolan,    ac sio hand gebarn
modiges mannes,    þær he his mæges healp,
þæt he þone niðgæst    nioðor hwene sloh,
secg on searwum,    þæt ðæt sweord gedeaf,
fah ond fæted,    þæt ðæt fyr ongon
sweðrian syððan.    þa gen sylf cyning
geweold his gewitte,    wællseaxe gebræd
biter ond beaduscearp,    þæt he on byrnan wæg;
forwrat Wedra helm    wyrm on middan.
Feond gefyldan    (ferh ellen wræc),
ond hi hyne þa begen    abroten hæfdon,
sibæðelingas.    Swylc sceolde secg wesan,
þegn æt ðearfe!    þæt ðam þeodne wæs
siðast sigehwila    sylfes dædum,
worlde geweorces.    ða sio wund ongon,
þe him se eorðdraca    ær geworhte,
swelan ond swellan;    he þæt sona onfand,
þæt him on breostum    bealoniðe weoll
attor on innan.

## English

Then I heard that at need of the king of the people
The upstanding earlman exhibited prowess,
Vigor and courage, as suited his nature;
He his head did not guard, but the high-minded liegeman's
Hand was consumed, when he succored his kinsman,
So he struck the strife-bringing strange-comer lower,
Earl-thane in armor, that in went the weapon
Gleaming and plated, that 'gan then the fire
Beowulf draws his knife,
Later to lessen. The liegelord himself then
Retained his consciousness, brandished his war-knife,
Battle-sharp, bitter, that he bare on his armor:
and cuts the dragon.
The Weder-lord cut the worm in the middle.
They had felled the enemy (life drove out then
Puissant prowess), the pair had destroyed him,
Land-chiefs related: so a liegeman should prove him,
A thaneman when needed. To the prince 'twas the last of
His era of conquest by his own great achievements,
Beowulf's wound swells and burns.
The latest of world-deeds. The wound then began
Which the earth-dwelling dragon erstwhile had wrought him
To burn and to swell. He soon then discovered
That bitterest bale-woe in his bosom was raging,
Poison within.

## 15.6 Quiz

### Translate from Anglo-Saxon to Modern English (1 point each)

1. rose — rose
2. sumor — summer
3. drygan — to dry
4. goma — gum
5. huntian — to hunt
6. furhlang — furlong
7. writan — to write
8. sunne — sun
9. swætan — to sweat
10. hearm — hurt
11. unsmeðe — rough
12. snofl — mucus
13. hnut — nut
14. ofercuman — to subdue
15. swapan — to sweep
16. spell — story
17. getwinn — twin
18. swimman — to swim
19. musle — mussel
20. saltere — psalter
21. streaw — straw
22. hat — hot
23. ofn — stove
24. crabba — crab
25. grund — ground

### Translate from Modern English to Anglo-Saxon (1 point each)

26. eye — eage
27. psalm-singing — sealmsong
28. storm — storm
29. bread — hlaf
30. sweat — swat
31. to cut one's hair — efsian
32. butterfly — buterfleoge
33. twenty — twentig
34. sword — sweord
35. guilt — gylt
36. to twinkle — twinclian
37. oyster — ostre
38. honeycomb — beebread
39. torment — morðor
40. string — streng
41. cucumber — eorðæppel
42. lung — lungen
43. purple dye — purpure
44. fuel — tynder
45. rough — unsmeðe
46. not at all — no
47. cunning — orðonc
48. worth — weorð
49. stich — stice
50. tusk — tux

[This page intentionally left blank]

## Fill in the blanks (50 points)

51.

**Hwæt! We Gar-Ðena** in **geardagum,**
**Þeodcyninga, þrym gefrunon,**
**hu ða æþelingas ellen fremedon.**
Oft **Scyld Scefing sceaþena Þreatum,**
**monegum mægþum, meodosetla ofteah,**
**egsode eorlas. Syððan ærest wearð**
**feasceaft funden, he** þæs **frofre gebad,**
**weox under wolcnum, weorðmyndum þah,**
**oð þæt him æghwylc þara ymbsittendra**
**ofer hronrade hyran scolde,**
**gomban gyldan. þæt wæs god cyning!**

# Chapter 16

# Unit Two - Final Exam 200 points

## 16.1 Vocabulary

### Translate from Anglo-Saxon into Modern English, or Modern English into Anglo-Saxon (50 points)

1. to suck — sucan
2. dragan — to drag
3. eternal cold — sincaldu
4. brimwylf — aquatic monster
5. provincial governor — ealdorman
6. mihtig — mighty, strong
7. to forswear — forswerian
8. ent — giant
9. today — todæg
10. hwæðer — however, whether, which of two, nevertheless
11. stronghold — burg, ceaster, fæsten
12. hwæt — hey! listen!
13. blow to the ear — earslege
14. middansumer — midsummer
15. to sweat — swætan
16. morgenleoht — morning light
17. sledgehammer — slecg
18. beebread — honeycomb
19. cider — æppelwin
20. sweord — sword
21. organist — organestre
22. hrim — rime
23. hilt — hilt
24. smiððe — smithy
25. vegetable — wyrt
26. hwistlung — whistling
27. story — spell
28. deaðscyld — capital offense
29. to hunt — huntian
30. gebedda — bedfellow
31. bible — biblioðece
32. bigspell — parable
33. wonder — wundor
34. hringedstefna — curve-prowed ship
35. snake — snaca, wyrm
36. wieldan — to wield
37. protector — helm
38. ealdfæder — ancestor
39. fort — burg, ceaster
40. deadboren — stillborn
41. course of events — wyrd
42. beogang — swarm of bees
43. district — scir
44. haligwæter — holy water
45. psalm-singing — sealmsong
46. Romeburg — Rome
47. cucumber — eorðæppel
48. sealm — psalm
49. murder — morðor
50. attorcoppe — spider

## 16.2 Translation

### Translate the following passage from Mark, after hiding your dictionary somewhere (89 points, approximately ½ point per word)

27 Ða eode he and his leorning-cnihtas on ðæt castel Cesareæ Philippi. And he on wege his leorning-cnihtas ahsode, Hwæt secgaþ men ðæt ic sy?

[Then he and his disciples went into the towns of Caesarea Philippi: and by the way he asked his disciples, What do men say that I am?]

28 Ða andswarodon hi, Sume, Iohannem ðone Fulluhtere; sume, Heliam; sume, sumne of ðam witegum.

[Then they answered, Some John the Baptist: but some Elias, and some, One of the prohets.]

29 Ða cwæþ he, Hwæt secge ge ðæt ic sy? Ða andswarode Petrus him, and cwæþ, Ðu eart Crist.

[Then he saith unto them, What say ye that I am? And Peter answereth and saith, Thou art the Christ.]

30 And ða bead he him, ðæt hi nænegum be him ne sædon.

[And then he bad them that they should tell no man of him.]

31 Ða ongan he hi læran, ðat mannes sunu gebyreþ fela þinga þolian, and beon aworpen fram ealdormannum, and heahsacerdum, and bocerum, and beon ofslegen, and æfter þrim dagum arisan.

[Then he began to teach them, that the Son of man must suffer many things, and be rejected of the elders, and of the chief priests, and scribes, and be killed, and after three days rise.]

32 And spræc ða openlice. And ða nam Petrus hine, and ongan hine þreagean.

[And he spake that saying openly. And then Peter took him, and began to rebuke him.]

33 Ða bewende he hine, and cidde Petre, and cwæþ, Ga onbæc, Satanas; forðam ðu nast ða þing ðe synd Godes, ac ða þing ðe synd manna.

[Then he turned about and rebuked Peter, and said, Go back, Satan: for thou do not know the things that be of God, but the tings that be of men.]

34 Ða cwæþ he, togædere geclypedre menegu, mid his leorning-cnihtum, Gif hwa wyle me fyligean, wiðsace hine sylfne, and nime his cwylminge, and folgige me.

[When he called the people unto him with his disciples also, he said, If anyone wishes to follow me, let him deny himself, and take up his cross, and follow me.]

35 Se ðe wyle his sawle hale gedon, se hi forspilþ; se ðe forspilþ his sawle for me and for ðam godspelle se hig gehælþ.

[He who wishes to save his soul shall lose it; he who shall lose his soul for me and for the gospel, the same shall save it.]

## 16.3 Memorization

### Write out the opening eleven lines from Beowulf into Anglo-Saxon (61 points, 1 point per word)

Hwæt! We Gar-Ðena in geardagum,
Þeodcyninga, þrym gefrunon,
hu ða æþelingas ellen fremedon.
Oft Scyld Scefing sceaþena Þreatum,
monegum mægþum, meodosetla ofteah,
egsode eorlas. Syððan ærest wearð
feasceaft funden, he þæs frofre gebad,
weox under wolcnum, weorðmyndum þah,
oð þæt him æghwylc þara ymbsittendra
ofer hronrade hyran scolde,
gomban gyldan. þæt wæs god cyning!